COMPANION

TO

ETHICS

A

PRACTICAL

COMPANION

TO

ETHICS

THIRD EDITION

Anthony Weston

Elon University

New York   Oxford
OXFORD UNIVERSITY PRESS
2006

Oxford University Press, Inc., publishes works that further Oxford University's objective of excellence in research, scholarship, and education.

Oxford   New York
Auckland   Cape Town   Dar es Salaam   Hong Kong   Karachi
Kuala Lumpur   Madrid   Melbourne   Mexico City   Nairobi
New Delhi   Shanghai   Taipei   Toronto

With offices in
Argentina   Austria   Brazil   Chile   Czech Republic   France   Greece
Guatemala   Hungary   Italy   Japan   Poland   Portugal   Singapore
South Korea   Switzerland   Thailand   Turkey   Ukraine   Vietnam

Copyright © 2006 by Oxford University Press, Inc.

Published by Oxford University Press, Inc.
198 Madison Avenue, New York, New York 10016
http://www.oup.com

Library of Congress Cataloging-in-Publication Data

Weston, Anthony, 1954-
A practical companion to ethics / Anthony Weston.—3rd ed.
p. cm.
Includes bibliographical references
ISBN-13 978-0-19-518990-2 (pbk. : alk. paper)
ISBN 0-19-518990-6 (pbk : alk. paper)
1. Ethics. I. Title.

BJ1025.W43 2006
170—dc22   2005051296

9 8 7 6 5 4 3 2 1

Printed in the United States of America
on acid-free paper

CONTENTS

PREFACE TO THE THIRD EDITION

Ethics continues to need help. It is no news that we could use a stronger sense of values. Less widely recognized is that ethics also needs certain other practical skills and attitudes: more open-mindedness, for example; more creativity; more willingness to listen and to reach across seeming differences to connect and make change together. Indeed, the need for these skills and attitudes has never been more pressing. They are the concern of this book.

Companion remains a brief book, though—still modest, I hope; still companionate; still intended chiefly as a supplementary book for college ethics courses, complementing the theoretical considerations that often consume such courses. Some of my colleagues use it to set the ground rules by which an ethics class will operate, especially in difficult discussions. Others use Chapters 1 and 2 to introduce the subject of ethics as a whole, take up 3 and 4 when the class turns to specific controversies, and return to 5 for a fare-thee-well at the end.

Either way, or any way, this book is also intended to be self-sufficient. Students can mostly read it and understand it on their own; it need not require a lot of classtime in courses that already may be too full.

From second to third edition there are several major shifts. Chapter 2 now focuses on ethics and religion, hoping to speak better to a situation in which mutual mistrust is rising and moral dialogue may seem especially fragile. Chapter 5 is redirected to highlight the continuously unfolding nature of ethical understanding. The Appendix is entirely rewritten and somewhat expanded, at the suggestion of several readers, to offer more practical advice about a wider range of possible kinds of papers. There are other small changes throughout.

Several other books of mine may interest readers who find this one useful. Students who want more on all of *Companion's* topics can turn to my *A 21st Century Ethical Toolbox* (Oxford, 2001). For an entire book dedicated to the theme of *Companion's* Chapter 3—creativity in ethics—see my new book *Creative Problem-Solving in Ethics* (Oxford, 2006). Teachers who want more on ethics and pedagogy should consult *Toolbox's* extensive Teacher's Appendix. For elaborations and defenses of some of the more philosophically controversial points, try my *Toward Better Problems* (Temple University Press, 1992).

As the number of editions of this little book grows, so too does my indebtedness to many friends, colleagues, and reviewers who have contributed advice, encouragement, and support. Though I did not always follow their advice, it was always appreciated. Peter Williams, Tom Birch, Nim Batchelor, and Scott Yost, along with Oxford's intrepid Robert Miller, helped shape and reshape the project from the beginning. Donald Becker, Earl Conee, Peter Markie, and several other philosophers served as publisher's reviewers for the first edition. David Boersma, David Detmer, Verna Gehring, and Ben Mulvey served in the same capacity for the second. For the third, my hat is off to Eric Dalton, Peter Dalton, Manyul Im, Robert Jensen, Elba Serrano, and Mark Smillie, with special appreciation to Joseph Cole, Douglas Groothuis, and Bob Kirkman. Thanks to you all! As always, I heartily welcome all readers' comments, criticisms, and suggestions.

A.W.
May 2005

INTRODUCTION

This book is an invitation to ethics. It is meant to fill the gap between the theoretical issues common in the ethics of philosophers and the practical questions of the doubter and the newcomer. One question is: who even *needs* ethics? Why think about values at all? Also, how do you come to terms with secular ethics if you've already got religion? These are real questions, and they need to be answered before the rest of ethics—its theories and its methods and its history—can speak to us.

This book also aims to bring out the connections between ethics and certain useful methods in practical thinking generally. For example, there is a large literature on creative problem-solving: on multiplying options and reframing problems so that the original problem is transformed. There is an equally large literature on conflict resolution and compromise, crucial skills if we are to avoid polarizing values and the people who hold them. This book brings all of these skills into the spotlight.

Finally, this book invites you to take up ethics in the spirit of an ongoing journey. Part of our task both practical and personal is to keep ourselves open to the complexities of real lives and to the world's own hidden possibilities. A little openness can go a long way. Some of the most intriguing developments in contemporary ethics begin right here. We could think of the emerging ethical awareness of other animals, for example, as one way in which the story of ethics continues to unfold in our own time.

This, then, is a *practical* companion to ethics. It is meant as an essential supplement to the usual first presentation of ethics, and an essential skill-book as one goes on in ethical practice. It invites, explains, improves, expands. It places ethics against a larger practical background, in order to clarify its role and its potential. It aims to uncover creative possibilities where we now seem to have only dilemmas and intractable conflicts. It seeks to open both our minds and our hearts.

It may seem odd that such book is necessary at all. Why can't the great theories of ethics, or the many textbooks and collected readings in ethics, explain ethics well enough by themselves?

The answer is complex—also controversial—and not something we can expand upon here. I will say only this. A better *invitation* to ethics is necessary because most of the main works in ethics tend to take the need for ethics for granted. This is not exactly an objection—the main works in auto mechanics and dance theory take the need for auto mechanics and dance theory for granted too—but it does leave gaps. A supplement can help. Otherwise ethics may seem too academic, or too much trouble. Why think for yourself, and invite social disapproval and uncertainty, when you can just take the word of the dominant authority figures? Why think at all, when we can just act out our feelings? Really, why?

Standard ethics books also seldom discuss the "how-tos" of ethics: how to frame a problem so that it can be most effectively solved; or how to deal effectively, interpersonally or politically, with fundamental ethical disagreements; or why and how feelings matter. Many philosophers prefer to concentrate on ethics' unique intellectual challenges. But most people come to ethics to learn how to *live*. This is a far broader question. By concentrating on certain intellectual challenges unique to ethics, we may slight the practical (and creative, and imaginative) skills that are vital to ethics but *not* unique to it. So part of the aim of this book is to rejoin ethics to life skills—to put ethics into its rightful place.

This book therefore does not duplicate the many histories and applications of ethics already available. It hardly mentions the usual theories and their advantages and defects and applications—that's for elsewhere. Instead, our concern here is with the practical skills that make ethics *work*, day to day, and can help it work better. Maybe dramatically better. And that is quite enough already!

Some of the advice offered in this book may seem obvious. If it does, just remember that we are much better at giving advice to others than at recognizing when we need it ourselves. Actually, we need the advice too, sometimes even the simplest advice. We need the reminders. Moreover, even when a mistake is "obvious," how to carry on in a better way—how to avoid the mistake next time around—may not be obvious at all. It may take some time and care to develop the necessary skills. Give them the time and the care that they need. They will repay your efforts many times over.

A

PRACTICAL

COMPANION

TO

ETHICS

1

GETTING STARTED

WHO NEEDS ETHICS?

Why isn't it enough to follow our feelings, or "fly by instinct," when we are thinking about what we should do or how we should live?

Feelings are essential, of course. A life without love, excitement, and even pain is no life at all. No liveable ethic denies this. But feelings are not the whole story. They may be the beginning, but they are not the end. A certain kind of *thinking* must also be part of the story.

Take prejudice. To be prejudiced is to have a strong negative feeling about someone who is of a different ethnicity or gender or age or social class (or . . .) from yourself. If ethics were just a matter of feelings, there would be nothing to say against such prejudices. It would be perfectly moral to discriminate against people you don't like.

Instinct says yes. Ethics says no. Ethics instead may challenge these very feelings. "Prejudice" literally means "prejudgment": it is one way of not really paying attention. But we *need* to pay attention. We need to ask why we feel as we do, whether our beliefs and feelings are true or fair, how *we* would feel in the other person's shoes, and so on. In short, we need to ask whether our feelings are *justified,* and, when not, what alternative feelings ought to take their place.

So ethics asks us to think carefully, even about feelings that may be very strong. Ethics asks us to live *mindfully:* to take some care about how we act and even about how we feel.

Consider another contrast with "flying by instinct." Instincts and feelings may oversimplify complex situations. We want things to feel clear-cut even when they are not, and so we may persuade ourselves that they are. Mindful thinking, by contrast, is more patient. Where things are really unclear, in particular, feeling may even have to wait. Premature clarity is worse than confusion. We may have to live with some questions a long time before we can decide how we ought to feel about them.

Our feelings are also easily manipulated. For instance, it is easy to be swayed either way by "loaded language," language that plays upon our emotional reactions. Define abortion as "baby-killing," and you create a negative feeling that closes the case against abortion before it really can even be opened. But a "fetus" is not a "baby" (look the words up). On the other hand, if you describe abortion as simply "minor surgery," you suggest that it is both unintrusive and even healthy. It isn't. Either way, we are led into a prepackaged emotional commitment without ever thinking it through. Habit and conformity take over.

Mindful thinking, by contrast, is more complex and open-ended. It is in this spirit that ethics approaches controversial

A FEW KEY TERMS

What *is* ethics, anyway? Philosophers and dictionaries often say something like this: ethics is *the study of moral values;* it considers *how best to think about moral values and how best to clarify, prioritize, and integrate them.*

This definition in turn draws on several others. What is a value, for one thing? In this book, by "values" I will mean *those things we care about; those things that matter to us; those goals or ideals we aspire to and measure ourselves or others or our society by.*

When we speak of "moral" values, we are concerned with a specific kind of values: *those values that give voice to the needs and legitimate expectations of others as well as ourselves.* "Legitimate expectations" may be of many sorts: we rightly expect to be treated with respect, for instance, and with honesty and care.

We often use the terms "ethics" and "morals" interchangeably. Still, it's often helpful to distinguish the moral values we happen to hold from the deliberate process of thinking them through, criticizing, and revising them. The term "ethics" has a more critical, self-conscious edge. Here we try to go beyond *living out* our values to *thinking them through.*

issues of the day, like abortion or professional ethics or the status of other animals. We do care for other animals, for instance. But we also use many of them for food, shoes, chemical tests, even as objects of sport. Should all of this stop? No? Well, should *any* of it stop? Probably. So what kinds of use of other animals should stop and what kinds should not? Why? How do you decide?

These questions cannot be adequately answered by just consulting your feelings. There are too many different possibilities, too many different "uses," too many different opinions and prejudices (on all sides) that need to be carefully sorted out. Again, it takes some time and care. Maybe even some degree of compromise.

Every moral issue discussed in this book is another example. I will try to suggest that much more intelligent and creative thinking is possible about these issues than we usually suspect. But the key word is "thinking." Ethics invites us to try.

THE DOGMATIST AND THE RATIONALIZER

Thinking is hard, though, and sometimes unpleasant. We may actually have to change our minds! As a result we have developed some pretty effective ways to avoid it. To get started in ethics we need to be warned against some of them.

Why Listen?

We all know the kind of people who are so committed to their moral beliefs that they cannot see any other side, and cannot defend their own beliefs beyond simply asserting and reasserting them—more and more loudly, probably. This is dogmatism. They may appear to listen (or not), but they *will not* change their minds. Name "their" issue (or perhaps *any* issue), and they know the answer already.

To be clear: being committed to a certain set of values—living up to them, or trying to, and sticking up for them when we can—is a fine thing. And there are certain basic moral values that we all share that we are and *should be* unshakeably committed to. Dogmatism is a problem because some people go much farther. They make no distinction between the basic "givens" of our moral life and everyday moral opinions that are not at all so clear-cut. Every one of their value judgments, to them, has the same status as the Ten Commandments.

Dogmatists tend to disagree about the actual issues, which in fact is a bit ironic. Dogmatists do agree, though, that careful and open-ended thinking about moral issues is not necessary. After all, if you already know the answer, there is no need to think about it. If you need to argue for your position, you admit that it needs defending, which is to say that people can legitimately have doubts. But that can't be true: you already know that your position is the only right one. Therefore, any reasoned argument for your position is unnecessary. And any reasoned argument *against* your position is obviously absurd. So, why listen?

Ethics, once again, paints a different picture. Despite the stereotypes, the point of ethics is generally not to moralize or to dictate what is to be done. The real point of ethics is to offer some constructive ways to think about difficult matters, recognizing from the start—as the very *rationale* for ethics, in fact—that the world is seldom so simple or clearcut. Struggle and uncertainty *are* part of ethics, as they are part of life.

It pays to adjust our language as well. Instead of categorical statements of dogmatic opinions, bumper sticker style ("Meat is Murder," "God is Pro-Life," etc., etc.), we need to try to speak in a way that is less categorical and final. Very few reasonable moral positions can be shoehorned into a bumper sticker or slogan, clever as they might be. Besides, this way of putting things polarizes views and makes the other side seem stupid and misled. Don't call names either ("You animal-rights fanatics . . ."; "You Bible-thumpers . . ."). Avoid the easy labels ("Liberal," "Right-wing" . . .).

Speaking in a more open-ended way may help you begin to *think* in a more open-ended way too. At the very least it will create quite different conversations! Typically one dogmatic statement just provokes an equal and opposite dogmatic statement. Speak differently and not only your mind but your discussions may open up differently, and more constructively too.

Offhand Self-Justification

I offer some view in a moral discussion. Someone challenges me. My natural first reaction is to defend whatever it was I just said, even if the challenge is exactly on target.

Call this "offhand self-justification." It is a kind of automatic excuse-making or defensiveness, or what we sometimes call "rationalizing." I may not even get to the point of asking if the challenge actually is on target. Indeed, that's the idea. I'd rather not. Self-defense is all that counts. I try to paper over my uncertainties (or insecurities, or half-knowledge, or wishful thinking) by grabbing for some excuse, and any excuse will do. "It's OK to cheat the phone company, because . . . because, well, everyone else does it too . . . because the phone company cheats *you* . . . because . . . ."

Asked for your reasons, you should give them. There is nothing wrong with trying to defend your view. The problem lies with the offhand or automatic spirit (or, more accurately, spiritlessness) of the defense. Once again, it becomes an excuse for not really *thinking*.

> S: Of course the death penalty deters murderers. It's a proven fact that murder rates are lower in states with the death penalty.
>
> A: I'm not so sure about that. My understanding is that most states with the death penalty have *higher* murder rates.
>
> S: Well, you can prove anything with numbers.

S initially appeals to "numbers"—comparative murder rates—to support her position. Challenged, though, she does not reconsider her position or explore other possibilities. She just dismisses any studies that disagree with what she believes, and in the process manages to dismiss the very "numbers" she herself just cited. But she doesn't notice. You can tell that in the next discussion she'll be right back citing the same "proven fact."

There are no surefire ways to avoid rationalizing. It takes a kind of self-confidence, honesty, and maturity, which develop slowly. Even then we seldom escape the temptation entirely. Sometimes it's hard to recognize an offhand self-justification when it is right in front of our eyes. Yet there are some useful strategies for overcoming the urge.

Keep in mind how self-defeating it is. When we make excuses to protect behaviors or opinions that really ought to be questioned and changed, we usually end up having to defend our excuses too. In this way we saddle ourselves with *more and more* unintelligent opinions—new ones invented, off the top of the head, to patch up the holes in the old ones. But the new ones are likely to be full of holes too. It's not a winning game.

Watch yourself. Step a little more slowly the next time you find yourself casting about for some excuse to put questions to rest. Ask instead whether you really are justified in the first place.

Watch for that telltale anger or irritation at being challenged. We often find ourselves becoming irritated or angry when our especially precious excuses are too persistently or effectively challenged. But of course, we get angry at the person challenging us, rather than considering that we might really be at fault for offering an offhand excuse in the first place. Better take the irritation as a warning sign.

Avoid the automatic counterattack. Again, watch yourself. Listening to someone else, are you trying to understand, or just waiting for the person to stop so that you can give your comeback? Are you trying to "win," or to learn? Watch your voice tone: are you conveying ridicule, irritation? Take a time-out if you need it. Give yourself some space to think.

ETHICS AND DIVERSITY

It's clear, day to day, that moral values vary. I think speeding is morally OK; you don't. Some societies tolerate homeless populations running into the millions; other societies find it shameful to allow even one person to live on the streets. Some cultures condemn sex between unmarried young people; others encourage it.

Recognizing differences like these can lead us to a useful humility. It helps open our minds a little. And it can give us some space, sometimes, to try to figure things out for ourselves. What's right for you may *not* always be right for me.

It is tempting, though, to go much farther. From our differences about moral values some people conclude that there is no way, or no need, to think carefully or critically about values at all. "It's all *relative*," people say. "Mind your own business." Maybe any moral opinion is really as good as the next. "Relativism" in this sense is often considered a threat or challenge to mindfulness in ethics. Is it?

Diversity and Common Values

Maybe not. For one thing, the diversity of values is probably overrated. Sometimes values appear to vary just because we have different beliefs about the facts. Maybe I am not bothered by speeding because I think it is perfectly safe, whereas you don't. But we both value safety in the same way. That's the basic value involved, and one that, in this case, doesn't vary.

How diverse are basic values? It's an open question. Some philosophers claim that ethics itself is framed by agreements about certain *very* basic values: not causing pain to innocent others, for example, or misleading others for your own ends. Every society must promote a certain degree of respect for others' lives and honesty in social and economic relations if it is to survive at all. Other basic values may still be "relative," though, such as the values attached to sex roles—one example of a kind of value that seems to vary a great deal among cultures. The relativity of values, then, may be somewhat partial, and as the values involved become more basic and more essential, they may converge too.

Besides, mostly we deal with people who share many of our values—and then once again thinking has a natural place to start. Maybe you and I cannot argue with, say, cannibals about the ethics of cannibalism. Maybe. But how often do you argue with cannibals? I have never argued with a cannibal, not even once, but I argue constantly with my own children, whose moral habits as well as eating habits also need some improvement. And I *can* argue with them—they are growing into *our* culture, and have some learning to do. Here, where most of our moral argument takes place, there's plenty of basis for going on together.

Diversity and Critical Thinking

Let us also look more carefully at those cases where values really do differ, even at the basic level. It doesn't automatically follow that thinking isn't needed in these cases. For one thing, we may still need to think more critically about our *own* values (the point of the first part of this chapter). There's plenty to learn anyway.

The same goes for our arguments or discussions with others. People disagree about all kinds of things (Is there life on

Mars? Did the butler do it?), but we don't suppose these other disagreements can't be resolved intelligently. In fact, disagreements usually provoke us to *more* critical thinking. Why not in ethics too? The fact that some people are racists, for example, doesn't prove that racism is only wrong "for us." It proves that people have some learning to do.

Thus, although relativism may appear to be the very model of open-mindedness, it actually can have just the opposite effect. It can *close* our minds instead.

> U: I support the death penalty. I believe that it saves lives because it makes murderers think twice before killing someone. Besides, the Bible says, "An eye for an eye, a tooth for a tooth."
>
> V: I don't agree.
>
> U: Why?
>
> V: I just don't. That's my opinion and it's as good as yours!

Maybe that's a little blatant, but you get the idea. Here relativism slides right into offhand self-justification. V treats it like a magic key to escape any kind of thinking whatsoever. She cannot be bothered to offer any reasons, let alone engage U's.

In fact, all opinions on this and most moral subjects require further thinking. Are U's arguments good ones? What values stand on the other side? What are V's reasons *against* the death penalty? Is the death penalty really a deterrent? Doesn't the Bible also tell us not to kill? Whether values are "relative" or not, there is no way out of some good hard thinking.

Diversity as the Occasion for Ethics

Sometimes, in fact, the very diversity of values creates the *need* for ethics. Certain decisions shape our lives together, and therefore affect all of us. Polluted air, for example, doesn't merely affect the polluters, or people who think pollution is morally unproblematic. All of us have to breathe it. Likewise, if our country joins a war effort or bans genetically modified foods or legalizes assisted suicide, all of us are to some degree affected. Or again:

D: I oppose legal abortion.

E: Why don't you just mind your own business? Like the slogan says, if you're against abortion, then don't have one!

But there is more to it than this. If some of us practice abortion and some do not, the result is a society in which abortion is practiced. The rest of us have to stand for it, at least insofar as we have to stand aside. In such matters, we cannot act as though everyone can simply do as they please without anyone else being affected.

The relativist's stock phrase "Mind your own business" is therefore an antisocial response. It not only lets the relativist avoid thinking: it also refuses to acknowledge that on issues like these, however much we differ, we still need to work out some intelligent way of going on together. These matters—certain basic moral issues—are not just your own business but *everyone's* business.

Some philosophers argue, in fact, that this is the very point of ethics: to help us arrive at certain standards that we all are to live by when all of us are affected by each other's behavior. On this view, ethics is precisely *for* those cases where "Mind your own business!" doesn't work as an approach to a problem—where we need to work things out together, however much we may differ. We still need to stay in touch, keep thinking, and keep talking. *That* is nothing less than ethics itself in practice.

FOR PRACTICE AND THINKING ~

Some Questions

We have noted some of the ways in which people close their minds, often without even noticing or admitting that that is what is happening. Now consider *yourself.* When do you get dogmatic? About certain issues more than others? Which ones? When do you tend to rationalize? When do you get defensive?

Give yourself some credit too. What are you *good* at hearing? On what topics are you truly open-minded? And why is this?

Hearing the "Other Side"

Name a moral position that you find especially hard to take seriously. Now challenge yourself to write or state this position in as neutral a way as possible. You don't have to be effusive, and don't try to be extremely positive—usually it is easier to be overpositive than to state a view carefully. Just try to state the position in a reasonable way. You may have to do some research to get it right. In class, ask a classmate who holds that position to help you out.

Consider also the *reasons* that are typically used to support this view. What are those reasons? What are the best reasons according to *you*—the reasons that would persuade you if any reasons could?

Again, don't argue with the position. Just look for the strongest defense of the position you can find. On the other hand, you don't have to *agree* with this position either—after all, you picked it because you not only disagree with it but find it hard to take seriously. The point is to try to understand it, and in general to try to get a little distance from your own reactions.

A Dialogue

Dogmatism, relativism, and various kinds of offhand self-justification are partly conversational or argumentative moves: that is, they occur in dialogue, in the back-and-forth of conversation or argument. Sometimes they are also subtle!

Carefully consider the following classroom dialogue and consider where (and why) you think it goes awry. How might a more open-ended dialogue on the same theme go?

F: Fighting racism and sexism used to be easier than it is now. It's harder to see what to do anymore. Affirmative action, for instance— it's just not so clear an answer.

G: I think it's clear. If Martin Luther King, Jr. were alive today, he'd be against affirmative action!

H: Why do you think that? He was *for* it when he was alive, wasn't he?

G: He always spoke up against what was wrong. I believe affirmative action is wrong, so . . .

J: No, it makes sense. This society is still racist and sexist, you know. And if you know someone is going to discount you because you're black or female, a little extra nudge just makes things equal again.

M: Well, you must be the exception that proves the rule. Everybody *I* know is against all those quotas!

L: I don't think they use quotas. They just check for biased patterns of hiring or school admissions over time.

M: And then what? Besides, how do you "check"? You have to use quotas!

L: Computers or something, I don't know.

P: It's discrimination either way. Either the racism or sexism J talked about, or reverse discrimination to correct past discrimination. Who's to say which is worse?

J: Oh give me a break! Colleges and universities already give preferential treatment to the children of alumni, and athletes, and even students from other parts of the country. What's the big deal about giving some preference on the basis of race or sex?

P: Right! It's all in your head. You're only discriminated against if that's how it feels to you.

NOTES

The view that values essentially reduce to feelings is sometimes called "subjectivism." The term "subjectivism," however, tends to have many different and even incompatible meanings, often depending on whether or not the person using the term agrees with the view being described. For a discussion and critique of various meanings of "subjectivism" in ethics, see the entry "Ethical Subjectivism" in the *Encyclopedia of Philosophy* (Macmillan and Free Press, 1967).

Rationalizing may be one of the deepest of all pitfalls in ethics (and probably in life generally), and deserves a chapter of its own in any fuller treatment. For some psychological background, including some fascinating and unsettling experiments, see David Myers, *Social Psychology* (McGraw-Hill, 2001), Chapters 2–4. For a useful overview of self-deception, see Chapter 19 of Mike Martin's *Everyday Morality* (Wadsworth Publishing Company, 2001).

There are almost as many characterizations of relativism as there are people who write about it. For a survey, see the articles on "Relativism" and "Moral Relativism" in *The Routledge Encyclopedia of Philosophy* (Routledge, 1998). Chapter 2 of James Rachels' *The Elements of Moral Philosophy* (McGraw-Hill, 2002) is a careful and accessible analysis of "the challenge of cultural relativism." On the prospect of common values across cultures, a good place to start is Sissela Bok's book *Common Values* (University of Missouri Press, 1995).

Beware of the temptation to interpret any kind of skepticism about or resistance to moral argument as some form of relativism. Take that common phrase, "Who's to say?," as in, "Who's to say that we should always tell the truth?" or "Who's to say that sex outside of marriage is always wrong?" This can certainly be a troublesome kind of challenge. Often its function is to put an end to a discussion that is just developing a useful critical edge. Many students, and their teachers too, therefore take it to be an assertion of relativism.

Yet it is not so clear that "Who's to say?" is really meant this way in normal use. Sometimes this little phrase may be just a way of resisting an appeal to authority in ethics—quite possibly a reasonable move. People need some space to think for themselves, and questioning the moral authority of those who make dogmatic or sweeping pronouncements may be a way to make that space.

Other times, what's taken for relativism may really be more like a recognition of the *complexity* of moral matters. Maybe, after all, there *is* no one single "right" answer to (many) moral questions—but not for relativistic reasons. It may just be that many moral situations are so complex that many different but equally good responses are possible. It does not follow that any answer is as good as the next (there are still plenty of *wrong* answers) or that critical thinking is pointless in ethics. Quite the opposite, once again: surely it would call for more flexible and subtle thinking still.

A useful website on many ethical matters is Lawrence Hinman's "Ethics Updates" site at <http://ethics.acusd.edu/>. Hinman's site covers a wide range of moral issues, and also offers a guide to other web-based ethics resources and a useful glossary of key terms in ethics. On relativism in particular, select the "Moral Relativism" box for articles and general definitions.

2

ETHICS AND RELIGION

Increasingly we are told that religion divides us on moral matters. You and your moral or religious community may have very strong beliefs about, say, same-sex marriage (or preventive war or human cloning or . . .), but then other people and *their* moral or religious communities may have quite different beliefs, just as deeply held and elaborately defended as yours. We seem to be stuck.

How can we negotiate ethical questions when such strong and insistent views come into play? Must the opposing sides just battle it out for the power to impose their distinctive truths? Or are there still ways to think together—between different religions and between the religious and the secular?

COMING TO TERMS

In fact there are ready ways to make progress together. The main thing is to seek *shareable terms and arguments*. And this is neither a mystery nor even very hard.

Moral Argument in a Diverse Society

We already know that when the conclusions of a specific group or community are carried into the larger society, they need to be put in shareable ways. Think of manufacturers who want tax breaks or soccer teams who want new fields or kids who want bigger allowances. *They're* persuaded already, of course, but when the task is to persuade the rest of us— legislators, consumers, taxpayers, parents—then we must be approached in terms of broader, shared values: fairness, maybe, or "common sense," or the overall social good.

The same goes for moral debates. Specific moral pronouncements (religious or not) do not have automatic authority in the larger society. Once again, some leaders or groups may be persuaded already, but when the task is to persuade others—*all* of us, in the broader and more diverse moral community that includes people of various religious backgrounds as well as nonreligious people—then the appeal must be to shared values. What are required are not pronouncements but *arguments*: giving reasons that actually address the listener, and acknowledging counterarguments. No side can simply insist on its way without careful and open-ended dialogue.

Although many non-Catholics admire the pope, for example, we are unlikely to take his word on family planning or the economy just because it is his word. Many Catholics don't either. Just like the rest of us, he has to *persuade*. In fact, the late Pope John Paul II was so effective for just this reason: he could reach across many differences not by appealing to his official religious authority, but by thoughtful argument and by example.

Working from Common Values

So look for shareable, general terms. In the larger, public debate, aim to speak not so much as Catholics or Muslims, agnostics or atheists, but instead as people united by certain basic values we are aiming to understand and put into practice together. We can still disagree, even sharply. There is room for argument. But frame your arguments using common values.

An inspiring example is the partnership between former South African President Nelson Mandela and South African Anglican Archbishop Desmond Tutu. Mandela is really a kind of moral saint, exactly the right leader for South Africa at a crucial moment of transition, who through his own life has been able to show a whole nation how to transcend the bitterness of past oppression. He is also a resolutely secular person. Tutu's lifelong struggle against apartheid, by contrast, has been from his pulpits, and the result is not only a stunning "Truth and Reconciliation" movement in South Africa—facing the past in order to move ahead together—but also in the wider world.

Two very different life paths, but common values still: one direction and one heart. Mandela and Tutu together have moved people of all stripes—religious and secular; Anglican and Jew and Catholic; political leaders and CEOs as well as ordinary folks—to action. If they could do it, in the face of such overwhelming odds, surely we can too.

Of course there will be times when we cannot find (enough) common terms. Sometimes you will find yourself challenged. On the other hand, if you *can't* make an argument work in common terms, maybe it is actually not so strong an argument after all. Here some caution is wise. As Chapter 1 put it, not every moral matter has the status of the Ten Commandments.

The Commandments themselves, though, really do lay out common values—values that others might "ground" in other ways, but common values nonetheless. No one is in favor of committing murder or bearing false witness or dishonoring your parents or lusting for what your neighbor has—even though we may sometimes do all these things anyway. There are many other common values too. Who wants to squelch hope, leave children in pain, or trash the earth? None of us. We can put it many ways, tell many stories, worship in a hundred different ways or not worship at all, but in the end, as to values like these, we are mostly on the same page. Start there.

LET THE STORIES BE STORIES

Certain biblical stories have become contentious too, with some groups claiming that certain stories have a single clear "moral"—a single truth about how we should live—while others draw different conclusions, and the nonreligious usually avoid them altogether. Once again it may appear that we're stuck.

Once again too, though, we can appreciate these stories within a broader understanding of moral argument that also requires us to acknowledge complexity and diversity—this time of interpretations. We'd be better off to consider that their truth isn't *simple*, and that, just as with conflicting moral arguments, no one moral story or interpretation of that story has automatic authority either. Still, they remain deep and suggestive—well worth thinking about.

Consider a particularly contentious one: the story of Sodom.

Two angels came to Sodom in the evening; and Lot was sitting in the gate. . . . When Lot saw them, he rose to meet them . . . and said, "My lords, turn aside, I pray you, to your servant's house, and spend the night, and wash your feet; then you may rise up early and go on your way." . . . He urged them strongly; so they turned aside to him and entered his house; and he made them a feast, and baked unleavened bread, and they ate.

But before they lay down, the men of the city, the men of Sodom, both young and old, all the people to the last man, surrounded the house, and they called to Lot, "Where are the men who came to you tonight? Bring them out to us, that we may know [i.e., rape] them." Lot went out of the door to the men, shut the door after him, and said, "I beg you, my brothers, do not act so wickedly.... Do nothing to these men, for they have come under the shelter of my roof. Behold, I have two daughters who have not known man; let me bring them out to you, and do to them as you please; only do nothing to these men, for they have come under the shelter of my roof." But [the crowd] ... pressed hard against Lot, and drew near to break the door. But [the angels] put forth their hands and drew Lot into the house to them, and shut the door. And they struck with blindness the men who were at the door of the house, so that they wearied themselves groping for the door. (*Genesis* 19:1-11)

God destroys the city the next day, after helping Lot and his family to flee.

So what *is* the true sin of Sodom? Some insist that it is homosexuality. And it's true that homosexual acts (of a sort) are in the story. Other verses can be cited in support of this reading as well. Nonetheless, the insistence that *the* sin *must* be homosexuality—that no other reading is even possible and that no other possible sin matters—misses the depth of the story itself. It's much less clear—and much more fascinating!—than that.

An ancient reading is that the true crimes of Sodom are its shocking level of violence and its extreme disrespect for strangers. That's certainly in the story too—in fact, one might have thought, a lot more central to it.

Ezekiel had another interpretation: "Behold, this was the guilt of ... Sodom: she and her daughters had pride, surfeit of food, and prosperous ease, but did not aid the poor and needy"

(*Ezekiel* 16:49). On this view, the story is really a call to social justice!

Moderns might suppose that if anything is specifically con-
demned in this story, it is rape. After all, rape is what the crowd
had in mind. It turns out that gang rape was a common practice of the times for humiliating enemies. So maybe *that* is the
true sin of Sodom—the readiness to sexualize humiliation?

We can't stop there either. Lot, who is presented as the only
decent man in Sodom, actually offers the crowd his own daughters in the place of his guests. The angels prevent these rapes
too from happening. But God still saves Lot from the destruction of the rest of the city. Does not Lot's treatment of his own
daughters offend God? Is the shelter of his roof for strangers
more important than the shelter of his home for his own children? We are reminded that this story was written at a time
when some values were very different than they are now:
when, for one thing, women were regarded only as a father's
or husband's property, for him to dispose of as he saw fit. And
it therefore becomes hard to take the story, whatever exactly
it condemns or doesn't condemn, as the moral last word.

In any case, again, the main point can hardly be said to be
clear. You begin to see why for some religious traditions—for
many Jews, for example—exploring multiple interpretations
of such stories is the core of the worship service itself. Reading the stories in this way is, once again, a shareable
approach—a kind of common ground. It's the opposite of trying to squeeze a single moral out of them, which barely is to
read them as *stories* at all. Let us approach them, together, as
the complex, many-layered narratives that they are.

THINKING FOR YOURSELF

As Chapter 1 argues, the first requirement of ethics is to *think*,
and to think appreciatively and hard, about moral matters. And

whether you are religious or nonreligious (or for that matter even a relativist!), you must ultimately think for *yourself*.

We know that we cannot plead that we are "just doing what we're told" by a political or military leader or a boss at work. It is still up to us to ponder and decide. But it is not just that such authorities are—for better or worse—unreliable. Moral philosophers hold that it is part of our very nature to reflect on moral consequences and ultimate values, to look at things from diverse perspectives, to reflect and to wonder. Kant and others argued that these capacities are the very ground of our own moral value. And most religious moralists agree. The traditional religious view is that by making us "in His own image," God gave us free minds and free will—so we are obliged to use them!

A Word from the Wise

Some people may find it hard to reconcile such a message with the experience of tight-knit religious communities in which the leaders fervently believe that they speak for God Himself and therefore *do* expect obedience. Critical thinking may be explicitly forbidden, and even when it is tolerated it is seldom understood or encouraged. Not only is it hard to buck such insistent and accepted authority, but also it can be hard to question leaders whom you rightly respect and may even love.

Still, though, there is a deep wisdom in what ethics asks. We can see this best by looking to the wisest of the wise. We have spoken of Nelson Mandela and Archbishop Tutu; I also think of Gandhi, the Islamic mystical poet Rumi, the original philosopher Socrates, just to name a few. These are great people. And they don't avoid moral issues—often they wade right in. They may *advise* us. They may attempt to *persuade* us, as may any respected and loved moral leader. But here is the crucial thing: none of these people would claim to speak for God or demand that you put their judgment in place of your own.

On the contrary, they are acutely aware of their own limits as well as the limits of others. They recognize that even with the best of intentions, they are still creatures of their time and place, and therefore *even they* will hear the voice of God (or however they might describe their moral perceptions) through the filters of partial understanding or the residues of local prejudice or the lack of the full range of human experience. So they lead by inspiring *more* thinking—not less.

God came to Elijah alone in the cave at Mt. Horeb. There, the Bible says, God spoke in a "still small voice" (I *Kings* 19:12)—a phrase that can also be translated as "gentle breeze," "soft whisper," "hardly a sound." A hiss, a rustle. There is a vital caution here. Hearing that voice can be a very tricky thing— and in any case it comes to each of us on our own. You begin to see why Quakers and many others, both religious and secular, have put their livelihoods and even their lives on the line for freedom of conscience—to heed the still, small voice within. Protestant Christianity itself began with the insistence that all people should be able to read and interpret the Scriptures for themselves. Thinking for yourself is not somehow irreligious. It is at the very core of the religious experience.

A Biblical Ideal

Thinking for yourself is also a biblical ideal. In fact, it turns out to be another theme of the Sodom story.

Just before the angels go to Sodom, they visit the patriarch Abraham in his desert tent. They declare God's intention to destroy Sodom if the rumors about it are true. But Abraham is troubled by this. He cannot see the justice of killing the innocent along with the wicked. So Abraham, says the Bible, "went before the Lord." He actually takes it upon himself to question God!

Abraham drew near and said: "Wilt thou indeed destroy the righteous with the wicked? Suppose there are fifty righteous within the city; wilt thou then destroy the place and not spare it for the fifty righteous who are in it? Far be it from thee to do such a thing, to slay the righteous with the wicked, so that the righteous fare as the wicked! Far be that from thee! Shall not the Judge of all the Earth do right?"

And the Lord said, "If I find at Sodom fifty righteous in the city, I will spare the whole place for their sake." Abraham answered, "Behold, I have taken upon myself to speak to the Lord, I who am but dust and ashes. Suppose five of the fifty righteous are lacking. Wilt thou destroy the whole city for lack of five?" And He said, "I will not destroy it if I find forty-five there." Again he spoke to him, and said, "Suppose forty are found there." He answered, "For the sake of forty I will not do it." Then he said, "Oh let not the Lord be angry, and I will speak. Suppose thirty are found there." He answered, "I will not do it, if I find thirty there." He said, "Behold, I have taken upon myself to speak to the Lord. Suppose twenty are found there." He answered, "For the sake of twenty I will not destroy it."

Then [Abraham] said, "Oh let not the Lord be angry, and I will speak again but this once. Suppose ten are found there." The Lord answered, "For the sake of ten I will not destroy it." And the Lord went his way, when he had finished speaking to Abraham; and Abraham returned to his place. (*Genesis* 18:23–33)

Abraham will not accept injustice even when God Himself proposes to do it. He goes to God—Abraham who acknowledges himself to be "but dust and ashes"—and questions and challenges. He even dares to call God to His own standards: "Shall not the Judge of all the Earth do right?"

Abraham certainly thinks for himself! Moreover, he is honored for doing so. God listens and answers. Indeed Lot himself was saved, the Bible says later, because God was "mindful of Abraham."

In short, thinking for ourselves is both a moral responsibility and a hard-won right. So the next time someone acts as though it is yours only to obey someone else's dictates, or even the dictates of God Himself (according to *their* intepretation, of course)—well, remember Abraham!

FOR PRACTICE AND THINKING ∼

Study!

Explore moral and religious frameworks other than your own. Talk to people from other traditions. And read. Learn how other people see things. You don't have to give up your own beliefs to do so, but you certainly will come back to them with greater understanding.

One good place to start is Peggy Morgan and Clive Lawton, *Ethical Issues in Six Religious Traditions* (Edinburgh University Press, 1996). On the foundations of ethics, two books that can usefully be put alongside each other are Scott Rae's *Moral Choices* (Zondervan, 1995), a conservative Christian approach to ethics informed by the philosophical tradition, and Kai Nielsen's resolutely secular *Ethics Without God* (Prometheus, 1990). There are further references in the notes to this chapter.

A Sufi Story

The text recommends reading Bible stories for their richness and depth. Certain religious traditions have been reading stories in this open-ended way for hundreds of years. Here is a lovely eight-hundred-year-old parable from the Sufi master Yusuf of Andalusia.

> Nuri Bey was a respected and reflective Albanian, who married a wife much younger than himself. One evening when he had returned home earlier than usual, a faithful servant came to him and said: "Your wife is acting suspiciously. She is in her apartments with a huge chest, large enough to hold a man. . . . It should contain only a few ancient embroideries. I believe that there may now be much more in it. She will not allow me, your oldest retainer, to look inside."

Nuri went to his wife's room, and found her sitting disconsolately beside the massive wooden box. "Will you show me what is in the chest?" he asked.

"Because of the suspicion of a servant, or because you do not trust me?"

"Would it not be easier just to open it, without thinking about the undertones?" asked Nuri.

"I do not think it possible."

"Where is the key?"

She held it up. "Dismiss the servant and I will give it to you."

The servant was dismissed. The woman handed over the key and herself withdrew, obviously troubled in mind. Nuri Bey thought for a long time. Then he called four gardeners from his estate. Together they carried the chest by night unopened to a distant part of the grounds, and buried it. The matter was never referred to again.

Try interpreting this one yourself. Is Nuri Bey's act a wise one? Does the story mean to suggest that it is? He doesn't push the point—he doesn't open the chest—but he apparently doesn't entirely trust his wife either. Or in burying the chest is his idea to also bury mistrust—is he still trying to avoid the "undertones"? Would his wife agree that he succeeded at this?

And—after all—what is in the box? Is it obvious that his wife is hiding a lover? Could it be something else—a present, maybe, that Nuri Bey is not quite ready for yet? Some other kind of magical possibility that his jealousy "buries" for him? Notice that for *her* the issue is trust. She withdraws "troubled in mind," but not in denial or defiance. What do you make of that?

For more such stories, see Idries Shah's collection *Tales of the Dervishes* (Penguin, 1970). The philosopher Martin Buber collected volumes of Hasidic tales in *Tales of the Hasidim* (Schocken, 1991). Back in *Genesis* and *Exodus*, meanwhile, every page has high drama. Here is Jacob cheating his brother out of his birthright, in turn to be misled and manipulated by his own children for the rest of his life. Here is Tamar seducing her father-in-law Judah— the same Judah who gives his name to half of the kingdom of

Israel, the same Tamar who is honored as an ancestor of King David and hence also of Jesus. Cain and Abel, Jacob wrestling the angel, Korach's rebellion—these stories are full of "undertones" too. The parables of Jesus are also often elusive and ambiguous, as his disciples constantly complain. (And don't you think it's interesting that the Bible reports this?) Keep exploring. . . .

God and the Good

Since Abraham asks, "Shall not the Judge of all the Earth do right?" he clearly does not think that values are literally defined by God's commands. If God's commands simply define the good, then "the Judge of all the Earth" does right *by definition*, and the question would be senseless. Many people find such a view troubling because it makes values seem arbitrary.

Instead, Abraham questions God Himself by independent or "natural" moral standards. This may seem troubling for other reasons. For one thing, how does Abraham *know* that it is wrong to kill the innocent, even if God Himself were to do it? Think about that question for a while. If you are reading this book in an ethics class, your readings may suggest some answers.

For another thing, if God does not define the good, then does the good in some sense define God? It may not surprise you that theologians and philosophers have been thinking about that question for several thousand years. Most, though not all, answer yes—in some sense. As to how this might be possible, ask your local theologian!

Modern believers also take it upon themselves to question and indeed disregard even the direct commands of God—indeed in such an everyday way that we hardly notice. Chapters 11 and 19 of *Leviticus* command us to avoid such "abominations" as eating shellfish and harvesting our fields to the very edges so as to leave none for the poor. These, like passages used to defend slavery (e.g., *Exodus* 21: 2–3, 7, 20–21), are usually dismissed as unfortunate by-products of a less enlightened time. The problem is that then it is difficult to cite *Leviticus* to condemn certain other "abominations," such as male homosexual intercourse (*Leviticus* 20:13). If we are going to claim that some of the direct commands in the Bible are outdated, then we can hardly claim that we simply have to accept others because they are, well, direct commands in the Bible. Aren't we necessarily back in Abraham's place, making judgments, as best we can, partly on our own?

NOTES

Citations in the text are from the Christian Bible (Revised Standard Version). On the Sodom story, remember that one meaning of "to know" is "to have sexual intercourse." Compare *Genesis* 4:1: "And Adam knew Eve his wife, and she conceived and bore Cain. . . ."

Compelling readings are Nelson Mandela's autobiography, *Long Walk to Freedom* (Back Bay Books, 1995), and Michael Battle's *Reconciliation: the Ubuntu Theology of Desmond Tutu* (Pilgrim Press, 1997). Mandela's "long walk" carried him from his birth in one of the leading families of the Xhosa people into the resistance movement as one of the founders of the African National Congress (ANC), in turn influenced by the revolutionary ideas of certain English nonconformists and Jewish immigrants and by South Africa's Indian community (both Hindu and Muslim) with its Gandhian traditions (Gandhi himself lived and worked in South Africa for twenty years). In a quarter-century of imprisonment Mandela and his fellow prisoners from all over the religious and revolutionary spectrum debated politics in the mine shafts, staged Sophocles and Shakespeare, read Xhosa poets and the atheist and pacifist Bertrand Russell, and on and on. You begin to see why in the end no single religious or ethical orientation was enough for them and thus what forged the ANC's distinctive vision of a multicultural and multireligious society, bound by a common goal and based on that "common ground" that Mandela describes as "greater and more enduring than the differences that divide."

The South African regime, throughout those long years, smeared the ANC as "godless" while appealing to the Bible to justify apartheid. Yet Mandela, characteristically, continues to speak appreciatively of religion. Religious schools educated him, for one thing—the regime at the time had no interest in educating blacks. And more:

> In a South African jail under apartheid, you can see a cruelty of human beings to others in a naked form. But it was religious institutions, Hindus, Moslems, leaders of the Jewish faith, Christians, it was them who gave us the hope that one day, we would come out, we would return. And in prison, the religious institutions raised funds for our children, who were arrested in thousands and thrown into jail, and many of them one day left prison at a high level of education, because of this support we got from religious institutions. And that is why we so respect religious institutions. And we try as much as we can to read the literature, which outlines the fundamental principles of human behaviour . . . like the [Bhagavad Gita], the Qur'an, the Bible, and other important religious documents.

Notice again: Mandela is not embracing any one of these religions—he appreciates them all. "Hope" is not sectarian. At times he himself uses religious language—for sometimes, surely, only the language of the sacred will do—but does not feel the need to take it very literally. Yet here alongside him stands his great colleague Tutu, who does. There are lessons in their ongoing collaboration for all of us.

Appeals to authority have long been a concern of philosophical ethics, going as far back as Plato's *Euthyphro*. Here Plato carefully analyzes the relation of the good to the gods and argues that an independent judgment of values is inescapable, even within religious ethics. For a contemporary discussion, see James Rachels, *The Elements of Moral Philosophy* (McGraw-Hill, 2002), Chapter 4.

A synoptic and constructive exploration of many of the themes of this chapter—starting with common values—is Joseph Runzo and Nancy Martin, editors, *Ethics in the World Religions* (Oneworld Publications, 2001). On the great Western quest for God, from the beginning to the present, start with Karen Armstrong's richly textured book, *A History of God* (Ballantine, 1993).

3

CREATIVE PROBLEM-SOLVING IN ETHICS

Many times we feel stuck when confronting a moral problem. Only a few options come to mind, none of them very appealing. In fact, our most immediate association with the word "moral" seems to be the word "dilemma." Moral *dilemmas.* We are supposed to have two and only two choices—or anyway only a *few*—and often neither choice is much good. We can only pick the "lesser of two evils." But, hey, that's life. Or so we're told.

Is it? In all seriousness: is it? How many alleged dilemmas are actually only what logicians call "*false* dilemmas"? How many times, when we seem stuck, do we just need a little more imagination? For one thing, mightn't there be some ready ways of multiplying options: of simply thinking up other possibilities, options we might not have considered? And how about rethinking the problem itself, so that it might be headed off in the future, or transformed into something more easily resolved? How much farther might we be able to go in ethics if we approached it with a little more creativity?

THE NEED FOR INVENTIVENESS IN ETHICS

Consider a famous moral dilemma: the "Heinz dilemma," from the psychologist Lawrence Kohlberg's research on moral development.

> A woman was near death from cancer. One drug might save her, a form of radium that a druggist in the same town had discovered. The druggist was charging $2000, ten times what the drug cost him to make. The sick woman's husband, Heinz, went to everyone he knew to borrow the money, but he could only get together about half of what it cost. He told the druggist that his wife was dying and asked him to sell it cheaper or let him pay later. But the druggist said "no." The husband got desperate and broke into the man's store to steal the drug for his wife. Should the husband have done that? Why?

Kohlberg used dilemmas like this to probe children's moral reasoning. He claimed that most children go through several different, markedly different, stages of moral reasoning. This is a much-debated theory, but that debate is not our concern here. Our question right now is just: is this a true dilemma or a false one? Does Heinz really have *no* options besides stealing the drug or watching his wife die?

I put this question to my ethics classes after they get a little training in creative problem-solving. Can they think of any other options for Heinz? It turns out that they can, easily. Here are some of their ideas.

For one thing, Heinz might offer the druggist something besides money. He may have some skill that the druggist could use: maybe he's a good house painter or piano tuner or a skilled chemist himself. He could barter, trading the use of his skills for the drug.

Or suppose Heinz called up a newspaper. Nothing like a little bad publicity to change the druggist's mind. Or to help the sick woman gain a few donations.

And why is the druggist so inflexible, anyway? Possibly he needs the money to promote or keep on developing his drug. But in that case Heinz could argue that a spectacular cure would be the best promotion of all. Maybe his wife should get it free! Or Heinz could buy *half* the drug with the money he can raise, and then, if it works, ask for the rest to complete the demonstration.

Then again: why we should trust the "miracle drug" in the first place is not clear. New life-saving drugs require extensive testing, which evidently has not happened yet in this case. Where's the Food and Drug Administration when you need it? Maybe the drug is not worth taking even if the sick woman could get it free. Or maybe she should be paid to participate in a drug test!

I sometimes lead creativity workshops for adults and give them the Heinz dilemma as well. They have wilder ideas still. Because the state is legally required to provide medical care for prison inmates, one group suggested that Heinz's wife break into the druggist's store herself and get herself arrested! Another group proposed that the *whole town* steal the drug, both making a moral statement and seeking strength in numbers.

So: Heinz *does* have alternatives. There are many more possibilities besides stealing the drug or watching his wife die. This is only a partial list, too. I am always delighted by each new group's ability to come up with new options; always there are a few I've not heard before.

I don't mean that there are no moral issues raised by Kohlberg's dilemma. There are. And of course (I add this point for philosophers) *if* one's goal in raising this dilemma is to illustrate the clash of certain ethical theories, or to make certain philosophical points, then it can be altered to foreclose some of the other options. Certainly some situations really *are* dilemmas. My point, however, is that it is a little too easy to accept alleged moral dilemmas without question, as if somehow dilemmas are the only appropriate or natural form for moral problems. Creative thinking is closed out before we even start. Narrow and limited questions leave us, not surprisingly, with narrow and limited answers.

HOW TO EXPAND YOUR OPTIONS

The practical question is *how* to think more creatively. *How* do we multiply options? It turns out that there are a number of very specific methods for more imaginative thinking, all of them as applicable in ethics as anywhere else.

Breaking "Set"

A little psychology is useful at the start. Our thinking is often limited by habits and unconscious assumptions that have worked well for us in the past. Psychologists use the word "set" to describe these habits and unconscious assumptions. (They're like concrete: at first they're fluid, but they quickly "set," and then we can't move.) "Set" can be so powerful that we literally cannot see any other options, even those right before our eyes.

Understanding "set" helps us appreciate some of the more unusual methods for expanding our options. To break "set" we need to loosen up, try something new, maybe even something that seems peculiar, embarrassing, or improbable. It may feel forced, but that's just the point: we're trying to force our way beyond our own habits.

Here is one method, probably the most obvious, and for that very reason the most commonly overlooked. *Ask around.* Listening to other people is not a bad idea anyway, just to understand them better and broaden your own horizons. Specifically in problem-solving, asking around (asking *anyone* else—friends, children, strangers on the bus, oracles . . .) is an excellent way to get new ideas—to break set. You don't have to follow their advice, but they can certainly give you a fresh perspective.

Brainstorming is another good method. Brainstorming is a process in which a group of people try to generate new ideas. The key rule is: defer criticism. It is tempting and "safe" to react to any new suggestion with criticism. In brainstorming we do just the opposite: we consider how some new idea *could* work, not why it probably won't. Even a crude and obviously unrealistic idea, passed around the room, may evolve into something much more realistic, and meanwhile it may spark other new ideas. Ideas can hitchhike on each other. Let it happen.

One further rule often used in brainstorming is that quantity is important. Some groups set quotas for new ideas and allow no criticism at all until the quota is met. This also helps new ideas to percolate and gives people room to think in an exploratory way, free from the fear of being criticized.

If you're still stumped, problem-solving expert Edward De Bono has another, truly wild suggestion. Go to the dictionary, or to any book for that matter. Open it to some page and pick

out a word at random—any word will do. Then see what associations that word suggests. Immediately your thinking has
a truly new stimulus. You are not just going around in the same
old circles. De Bono calls this method *random association.*

Once again it may seem silly. Once again, though, some such
stimulus is just what we need in order to break our "set." We will
still need to work on the new ideas once we've found them, but
random association is a wonderful way of generating them.

In the face of the Heinz dilemma, for instance, you might
turn to the dictionary for random associations. When I did it,
the first word I found was "oboe." "Oboe?" I said to myself.
"You've got to be kidding!" Then I thought: Well, an oboe is a
musical instrument; an oboe-like instrument is used to charm
cobras in India; maybe Heinz could somehow charm the druggist? How? Well, I'm not sure, but it seems like a good idea for
Heinz at least to talk to the druggist again.

Back to oboes. People play such instruments; people have
skills; Heinz has skills: aha! From here we might begin to think
about bartering skills for the drug. The next word I found was
"leaf." Leaf: "Turn over a new leaf"? "Read leaves"? (Hmm—
foretelling the future, as people used to do with tea leaves?
How do we know that this drug is any good . . . ?) Maybe Ms.
Heinz should use leaves instead of drugs. (Are there herbal
remedies . . . ?). Do you see how thinking begins to loosen up?

The Intermediate Impossible

Yet another possibility: De Bono proposes a method he calls
the *intermediate impossible.* If you have a problem, start by
imagining what would be the perfect solution. Quite probably the perfect solution would be too costly, or physically impossible. But don't stop there—don't just give up and go back
to where you started. Work backward slowly from what's
perfect-but-impossible toward "intermediate" solutions that

are possible, until you find a possibility that is realistic. In short, make your very first step a big and wild one—otherwise you may never take a big step at all.

Think for example of the problem of speeding—people driving faster than the speed limit, to the point that other drivers are endangered. It's both a moral issue and a practical one. And we know the usual option: ticket more speeders. Couldn't there be others?

What would a "perfect" solution be? How about: cars that actually *can't* speed—cars that just don't go that fast. This kind of built-in constraint isn't realistic, I suppose, because people sometimes need to go extra fast: in emergencies, for instance, or when passing on two-lane roads. But this first and unrealistic idea may lead us to others that might be practical. For example, what about cars that automatically sound a siren or flash lights when they go too fast? Speeding would still be possible, then, but it would also be immediately evident to everyone. (Apparently Singapore actually has taxis like this.) You and I would know whom to look out for; the police would know whom to stop.

Or maybe we could build speed constraints into the roads themselves. Suppose special undulations were designed into road surfaces so that cars begin to vibrate unpleasantly when the speed limit is exceeded. Then roads could enforce their own speed limits!

Also "perfect" would be if people simply didn't want or need to speed in the first place. This suggests at least one good "intermediate" solution: to try to reduce the *pressures* to speed. For instance, some people speed because they are compelled to make it to work at a particular time regardless of traffic or weather or family needs. It might be better to let workers' work day begin whenever they arrive, so that they needn't rush to start at a fixed time. This would give us a lot more flexibility in the rest of our lives as well.

The "intermediate impossible" can lead to dramatic and competely unexpected new ideas. It can also move us decisively beyond the tendency to just complain about a problem, or to stick to our side in a fight, without making any progress. When we actually arrive at an idea of what we *want*—not just what we don't want—we sometimes discover that it is not so different from what "the other side" wants. Or not so different from what we've got already.

You see, anyway, how new ideas arise. They are there to be found: the crucial step is to *look*. Confronted with two or three bad choices and the demand to make a decision, start brainstorming. Free-associate. Ask around. Get out your dictionary. Don't let anyone tell you that you have no other options. You can't find out until you start looking for them.

HOW TO REFRAME PROBLEMS

A more radical approach is often possible too. There is a particular kind of set I call "freezing the problem." We freeze a problem when we act as though all we can do is to cope with the problem, accommodate ourselves to it, react after it has happened. Suppose, though, that the problem itself can be changed, made less serious, or even eliminated. The key question might be: what about trying to prevent the problem from even coming up? What about thinking preventively, so that in the end there is no problem left at all?

Some friends of mine loved to have fires in their fireplace. But they lived in a house so designed that when they wanted to use the fireplace, they had to haul firewood through the whole house to get it there. The result was that they seldom built fires, and when they did they made a huge mess. For years they just tried to carry wood more carefully. Later they were proud of themselves for hauling wood in a box, to avoid dropping splinters and dirt all through the house. But this was awkward too. The halls were still small, the box large.

No doubt there were still more creative options: maybe getting wood cut into really tiny pieces, or buying the dirt-free fake logs you see in hardware stores, or getting some nice dirt-colored carpet so the mess was less noticeable. Once again, however, notice that all of these ideas left the problem as it was. They froze the problem rather than changing it. Suppose that instead we ask: Is there a way to prevent this problem from even coming up?

A precocious cousin finally suggested that they knock a hole in the wall right next to the fireplace and put in a little door and a woodbox. My friends were delighted and did just that. Voila—end of problem!

My friends missed an obvious and simple alternative because they were preoccupied with better ways to haul wood through the house. They were becoming very good at accommodating themselves to a badly designed house, when in fact they needed to *change* the house. Odd as it may sound, "solving" problems is not the only way to deal with them! Sometimes it is not even the best way. Notice that my friends did not actually solve the problem of how to haul wood through the house without making a mess. They simply eliminated that problem. Now they don't haul wood through the house at all. There is no problem left to solve.

Preventive Ethics

Faced with a moral problem or "dilemma," then, one fundamental question we need to ask is whether the problem itself can be changed, made less serious, or even eliminated. We need to look at the bigger picture, at the roots and causes of such problematic situations, and ask what we can do about *them.*

Kohlberg has us worry about whether Heinz should steal a drug that is necessary to save his dying wife. Maybe Heinz can find some other way to save his wife or get the drug. But there is a range of more probing background questions that Kohlberg does not ask. Why does the sick woman have no insurance? Why can't public assistance help her? If either insurance or public assistance was a real option, Heinz's dilemma would not come up in the first place.

We have learned to ask what should be done when the family of a person in a "persistent vegetative state" wants her respirator turned off. Now let us learn to ask the background questions, like why nobody knows her wishes on the subject, or why the hospital's lawyers have the last word. Why not mandate much clearer "living wills"—a person's declaration of her desires about what she wishes done should she become comatose, made while she is still of sound mind? Why not take end-state care out of hospitals entirely and back to hospices or even homes, where families have the last word?

Executives and managers worry about whether whistle-blowers are being disloyal or destructive, while consumer advocates worry about how to encourage and protect them. But what about the preventive questions? How could the need for whistleblowing be prevented in the first place? Some reformers propose much more effective ways of protecting lines of communication and complaint within corporations and bureaucracies, thereby reducing or eliminating the need to go public with disruptive and controversial accusations, ruining one's own professional life and possibly those of others along the way. Others have suggested more effective public participation in large corporations, so that abuses become less frequent. Some experiments have been tried along these lines. We need to pay more attention. The possibility of such reforms is every bit as much an answer to the problem of whistleblowing as the usual hand-wringing about the conflicting values of loyalty and honesty and such. Why let such conflicts become so intense in the first place?

We worry about "the drug problem." But all we usually see are offenders—dealers and users—and all we usually consider is punishment: jail, mandatory sentencing, more police. Once again a whole range of constructive possibilities is being ignored. There are truly fundamental questions here, like why people are attracted to drugs in the first place, and why it is so difficult to get free later. Surely part of the appeal of drugs, at least initially, is that they offer some excitement in the midst of an otherwise uninteresting life. Then one bottom-line question is: are there less lethal ways to make life more interesting? Yes, obviously. Well, *what* ways?

Now there's a fine question! What can we do to make life so interesting that people are no longer tempted to escape through drugs? A truly "better problem": no longer punitive, widely engaging, promising for all of us.

Of course, problems cannot always be reframed. Sometimes there is no time. Heinz, for example, may have very few options left. A person on a respirator in a hospital is already quite thoroughly "framed." There may be some moral questions that cannot usefully be reframed even if there is time. The point, though, is that we tend to overlook even the *possibility* of reframing our problems. Don't simply assume that reframing is impossible, and resign yourself to just shouldering the same old burdens. Raise your head a little; look around; give yourself some room to move.

"Opportunism"

Albert Einstein once said that every difficulty is also an opportunity. Suppose we take him at his word. Could *moral* problems also be opportunities, rather than simply problems to be solved or even eliminated? Could it be that we can make use of what *seems* to be a problem in some new and unexpected way?

Here's a problem: if you go to any nursing home or assisted-living center, you will find people desperate for something constructive to do. There are some organized games and other activities, but the overall feeling is just that time is being filled. Professionals are even trained and hired to find ways to keep the residents busy—disguising what we normally assume to be the simple fact that really there *is* nothing for them to do. There is no one even to hear their stories.

You could look at this situation and see only a difficulty: how to fill up elderly people's time. You could also look at the very same situation and see an opportunity. Here, after all, are a large number of experienced people who have certain physical limits but who nonetheless have time, love, and experience to pass on. Couldn't anyone use a little of that?

Of course! What about children, for example? Many parents are desperate for good-quality child care, for a setting in which children can be cared for and can learn and grow into the larger community in richer ways than they might at home. And therefore, right now, in another building possibly quite near the assisted-living center, professionals are once again trained and hired, this time to find ways to keep children busy and maybe even teach them something. And once again we normally assume that there is nothing especially constructive for the children to do either. Just "play," or, in the cheaper day care centers, watch TV.

Mightn't precisely the neediness of *both* groups also have its hidden opportunities? Can't we make one solution out of two problems? Why not bring the very young and the very

PROBLEM-SOLVING STRATEGIES AT A GLANCE
To expand your options: • Ask around • Brainstorm (i.e., in a group, generate a set number of ideas *without criticism*) • Use random or free association • Seek the "intermediate impossible" To reframe your problem: • Think preventively (are there ways to keep the problem from even coming up in the future?) • Ask: Is the problem also in some way an *opportunity*? (And then: for *what*?)

old *together* in a setting in which both can help each other? The old can tell their stories to the very people who love stories above all. And the young can help tend to the needs of the old, learning something of life cycles and of service in the process. In every traditional society in the world the old are the ones who initiate the young into the life and history and stories of the culture—and the young are not shielded from the fears and losses that the end of life brings. They help out. What they could offer each other!

This idea is what De Bono would call a "raw" idea—the beginning of something truly creative, with the details still to be sorted out. It needs work. Fine. Examples like these give you at least a glimpse of what really might be possible. Even our *problems* have creative possibilities!

FOR PRACTICE AND THINKING ⁓

Problem-Solving Practice

To limber up your creativity, practice the methods in this chapter all the time, not just in ethics. Bored? Challenge yourself to figure out ten, or twenty, new and different uses for some everyday object, like a brick. Yes, it can be a paperweight or a doorstop or a shelf support. What else? Suppose you tape on a return-postage-guaranteed junk mail reply form and drop it in a mailbox—a good way to protest junk mail. Suppose you leave it in your yard until you want to go fishing, and then collect the worms underneath. Suppose . . .

Or again: What can you do with a . . . cheap ballpoint pen (besides write)? . . . a piece of paper? . . . a rotten apple? . . . a bad joke? When you get stuck, use the methods from this chapter!

Now pick some specific practical problems around your school or area and challenge yourself to add to (let's say, triple or quintuple) the number of options usually considered. For practice, they needn't be moral problems. Try problems like waste (Styrofoam cups, lights left on all the time, newspaper, etc.); alcoholism and other addictions; too much television; lack of inexpensive travel options; alternatives to on-the-air fund raising for public radio; parking issues at school or elsewhere; or low voter turnout. A look at any newspaper will produce many more. Don't forget to try to *reframe* these problems too. How might you prevent them from even coming up? And what might too much Styrofoam or too little parking space be an *opportunity* for?

Moral Problems

Now consider more familiar moral issues, and use the option-multiplying and reframing methods as you did with the practical problems just mentioned. Once again, challenge yourself to triple or quintuple the number of options usually considered.

This will feel awkward at first—it seems not quite serious enough an approach for moral issues, which we're always taught must be serious indeed. Try them anyway. Get used to it: give the methods a chance to show what they can do.

What alternatives might there be for a convicted murderer, for instance, besides capital punishment or life in prison? I expect that you can think of four or five serious options in five minutes if you apply yourself. And while you're at it, what about that seemingly hardest of our current moral issues—abortion? Give that one some real thought: I will tell you in advance that there's a *lot* that can be done with it with even a little creative thinking.

Don't settle for an idea that's only a *little* bit different from the usual. The methods in this chapter can take you farther than that. Get wild!

NOTES

For more on these and other creative problem-solving methods, see my *A 21st Century Ethical Toolbox*, Chapters 11 and 12, and my new book, *Creative Problem-Solving in Ethics* (Oxford University Press, 2006). For a general introduction to problem-solving broadly conceived, see my *Creativity for Critical Thinkers* (Oxford University Press, 2006), Marvin Levine's *Effective Problem-Solving* (Prentice-Hall, 1993), and the many works of Edward de Bono, such as *Lateral Thinking* (Harper and Row, 1970).

As I say in the text, one can certainly redescribe the "Heinz dilemma" or other examples to cut off each new option as it comes up, so that finally Heinz must "just choose." If your purpose is solely to illustrate the clash of different ethical theories, this may seem to be a natural move, and trying to come up with new options may indeed seem to confuse things, even to miss the point. And of course there *are* genuinely hard choices. Nonetheless, there are often other options too. We need the encouragement—more than we usually get in ethics texts—to look for them, to avoid locking ourselves into unpromising problems.

From a philosophical point of view, moreover, the possibility of creatively rethinking moral problems raises the question of the very nature of moral problems. If moral problems are like puzzles, distinct and well defined, then it does "miss the point" to try to rethink them creatively. Pragmatic philosophers, though, argue that moral problems are more like large, vague regions of tension, not at all distinct or well defined. "Problematic situations," Dewey called them. No "solution" can really be expected. They are also, for just the same reason, regions of opportunity. Constructively engaging the problem—trying to change it into something more manageable, making something of the opportunities—is the most intelligent response, and often the *only* intelligent response.

For further discussion of these points, and an extended argument for the last claim, see my book *Toward Better Problems* (Temple University Press, 1992). For Dewey's view, see James Gouinlock's collection *The Moral Writings of John Dewey* (Macmillan, 1976). The term "preventive ethics" is Virginia Warren's: see her essay "Feminist Directions in Medical Ethics," *Hypatia 4* (1989) and my discussion in *Toward Better Problems,* pp. vii–viii, 24–28, and 183.

The Heinz dilemma is cited from Lawrence Kohlberg, "Stage and Sequence: The Cognitive-Developmental Approach to Socialization," in D. A. Goslin, ed., *Handbook of Socialization Theory and Research* (Rand McNally, 1969), p. 379. For a critique of Kohlberg's conclusions see Carol Gilligan, *In a Different Voice* (Harvard University Press, 1983), pp. 27–38. There is an extended discussion of the Kohlberg–Gilligan debate in Eva Kittay and Diana Meyers, eds., *Women and Moral Theory* (Rowman and Littlefield, 1986). Astonishingly enough, subjects in Kohlberg's studies were graded as morally "immature" if they started exploring other possible options for Heinz. The researchers concluded that these subjects just didn't understand the dilemma. In fact, I think, they understood it better than the researchers. They understood it as a *false* dilemma, which is exactly what it is.

4

Don't Polarize—Connect

Our moral values often diverge. Sometimes they stand in painful opposition. Sometimes they are just imperfectly compatible, or pull in different directions. Either way, divergence can be a practical problem. We need to decide how to go on when we ourselves feel divided, and we need to be able to go on together when our values diverge from those of others. One of the major tasks of ethics is to offer some help doing so.

"RIGHT VERSUS RIGHT"

One problem is that we often exaggerate our divergences, making them much worse than they might be. We *polarize* values.

Look around at the bumper stickers you see on major moral issues. On most of these issues there are usually supposed to be just two, clearly distinct and opposite positions. On abortion, "pro-life" sets itself up against "pro-choice," and vice versa. On gun control, assisted suicide, gay marriage, and a host of other hot issues, it's often just "yes or no." Almost no other options get discussed. *Time* magazine did a famous cover about the standoff between timber interests and endangered spotted owls in the Pacific Northwest: they labeled it "Owl versus Man." Once again: no ambiguity, no gray areas, no middle ground. Sharp, dramatic, bitter—it makes a good headline.

Polarizing values has another side too. We usually suppose that one side—our own, of course!—is completely right and the other side completely wrong. We polarize values in order to picture ourselves as totally justified, totally right, and the other side as totally unjustified and totally wrong. All good on one side, all evil on the other. Day and night, black and white, us and them. Polarizing values therefore makes things crystal clear, protects us from doubts, justifies us completely. Our choices become easy.

But polarizing values is a bad idea. Reality is more complicated, more interesting, and maybe, just maybe, much more promising.

In nearly every serious moral issue, the truth is that both sides have a point. Or rather, *all* sides have a point, since there are often more than two. All sides speak for something worth considering. Each side is right about *something*.

To put it another way: most moral conflicts are real, not just mistakes by one side or the other about what really matters. There is genuine good on *both* sides—on *all* sides. "Only dogmatism," wrote the philosopher John Dewey, "can suppose that serious moral conflict is between something clearly bad and something known to be good, and that uncertainty lies wholly in the will of the one choosing. Most conflicts of importance are conflicts between things which are or have been satisfying, not between good and evil."

Again—they are choices between one good thing and another. Not "right versus wrong" but "right versus *right.*" We need to start by honoring that fact.

PIECES OF THE PUZZLE

Suppose that we try a new tack in approaching moral debates. Instead of asking which side is right, let us ask what *each* side is right *about.* That is, instead of approaching any other view looking for its weak points (according to us), start the other way around. Look for its strong points. Assume that it has some; the challenge is to find them. Even moral arguments that make absolutely no sense to you do make sense to others who are every bit as intelligent and well intentioned as you. There's got to be *something* in them. Figure it out.

What Is Each Side Right About?

Take the "assisted suicide" debate. The question is: should doctors be able to assist certain people to enable their own dying— say, people who are approaching death or total disability and are in great pain?

One side says yes: assisted suicide may be the only way in which some people can finally escape their unrelenting pain. Besides, we are free individuals entitled to make that choice.

The other side says no: allowing and perhaps encouraging doctors to kill, or even just to assist in death, takes a step toward devaluing life, and who knows where it will lead. Life is precious even in pain.

This is a difficult matter, for sure. But it is difficult precisely because both sides have valid points. Freedom from pain matters, and autonomy matters, and also respect for life matters. *Both sides are right.*

Most of us can spell out the values on both sides of an issue like this if we give it some thought and take care to avoid oversimplifying the issue. It just takes some exploring, with at least a somewhat open mind. Doing a little research, maybe. Listening, actually *listening,* without worrying about our "comeback," to what people on other sides are saying. Reminding ourselves that they have some pieces of the puzzle too. So do we. But it's very unlikely that any of us have the whole picture all by ourselves.

What Is Each Theory Right About?

Perhaps you already know something about traditional ethical theories or moral systems, or perhaps you are are studying them now. They can help too. Ethical theories such as theories of rights, for example, give us a way to express and connect values. It's often a helpful question to ask what specific rights are at stake, on either or both sides, in a problematic moral situation. In the case of assisted suicide, for instance, one right with which we surely have to come to terms is each person's right to make fundamental, life-or-death choices for themselves. That's part of the puzzle too.

Ethical theories or moral systems may also give us unexpected and deeper insight into a problem than we had before. The philosopher Immanuel Kant proposed a striking way to think about suicide. "If [we] kill [ourselves] in order to escape from painful circumstances," he wrote, "we use a person [ourselves] merely as a means to maintain a tolerable condition to the conclusion of life." Once life offers us no more pleasure we conclude that our life has no more value. But this move, so very natural if you think just in terms of pleasures and pains, is for Kant a fundamental mistake. Our lives, he argues, have value *in themselves,* not just as a means to something else, even of our own. We must respect our *own* lives just as we must respect the lives of others around us.

A subtle point—yes. Subtlety is part of what ethical theories have to offer. They can help us to see farther, and to see more, than we could see without them.

Once again, though, it doesn't follow that only one such theory is right. Rather than ask *which* theory is right, we need to ask instead, once again, what *each* theory is right *about.* We're not necessarily stalemated if we can't choose between them—that's only if we assume that we have to finally go with just one. But we don't. Each highlights certain values pushed into the background by the others. Just like the different "sides" in the popular debate, each has a *part*—but still only a part—of the puzzle.

GOING AHEAD TOGETHER

Probably the chief reason we hesitate to acknowledge right on both (all) sides of a moral debate is that we're afraid that then we'll be unable to do or decide anything. If both sides are right, what can we *do?* How can we possibly resolve the question, move ahead? Won't we then just be stuck?

No. There are many ways of going on from the acknowledgment that both (all) sides have a point. In fact, people who deal regularly with conflict resolution usually insist that only such an acknowledgment makes it *possible* to go on constructively. Moreover, most of the conflict resolvers' methods are familiar. All of them are so eminently sensible that nothing in this section will be a surprise—though I hope it may be an inspiration. The task is to put them to use *in ethics.*

Practical Strategies

Specifically, the task is to *integrate* the values at stake. If both sides (or all sides) are to some extent right, then we need to try to honor what is right in each of them. We need to try to answer to *all* of the important values at stake, rather than just a few.

This is a lot less difficult than it may sound. In fact, we do something of the sort constantly.

Suppose that for our summer vacation my partner wants to go to the beach and I want to go to the mountains. We could just battle it out, or flip a coin, and end up doing one or the other. That's how it goes sometimes—a "win/lose" battle.

A little better would be to compromise, to "split the difference." Maybe this year the beach, next year the mountains. Or maybe we could do a little of each this year. Though compromising is sometimes treated as disgraceful or weak willed, here it seems to be quite the opposite: a clear-headed acknowledgment of the diversity of values at stake, and an attempt to answer at least partly to both of them. Simple.

But we can do far better still. Suppose that she and I try to figure out *why* we want to go to the beach or the mountains. Maybe it turns out that she wants to be able to swim and sunbathe, and I want to be able to hike. These goals are not incompatible at all. There are some great lakes in the mountains, and some great hiking trails near the ocean. Both of us can have exactly, or almost exactly, what we want, and at the same time too.

Or suppose tonight my daughter and I are at home and she wants quiet and I want music. It would be crazy for us both to insist that only *our* desire is "right" and fight it out until one of us gets just what we want. Why not just have music for a while and then quiet? A little of both. Or we can work in different rooms. Or I could get a pair of earphones, in which case we could both have *exactly* what we want. Here we move beyond mere compromise to a truly "win/win" solution. It may turn out that our competing desires aren't incompatible at all.

Moreover, sometimes when we really look into the values on the "other" side, we recognize that some of them are not just compatible with our own but in fact are the *very same* values we hold ourselves. Though we tend to focus on our disagreements, normally there are background agreements that may be far more important. For example, in the vacation question, my partner and I agree from the start that we want to spend our vacation outside, in nature. It may be that the exact location matters much less than simply being outside together, and being physically active. Suppose that we started our negotiation there, on common ground. Basically, once again, we're on the same page. We're in it together. Only the details need to be worked out.

Assisted Suicide

Now let us come back to moral issues to put these strategies to work. Take the assisted suicide debate. Is there a space for the creative integration of values here? I think so.

For starters, both sides agree about something basic: that it is a very bad thing to suffer such pain that death seems appealing by comparison. That is clear and central common ground.

Right away, then, the possibility of reframing the problem suggests itself. What can we do to make the end of life less painful? What about developing super-powerful painkillers? What about removing the barriers that still block some dying people from using massive amounts of morphine or other painkillers that would be addictive or otherwise harmful if used by healthy people?

There's more. It turns out that it is not always the pain that makes people seek assisted suicide. Some of my students found a website that included biographies of the people that Dr. Jack Kevorkian—the famous (some say infamous) freelance crusader for assisted suicide—has helped to die. Though it was a pro-Kevorkian website, the students began to realize that Kevorkian became a last resort for many people because they were not only in pain but also lacked any kind of family or social support. They felt helpless, useless, and abandoned.

Neither side would say that in this kind of case the right answer is death. The real answer is to create communities of care such that people are not abandoned in this way. That's a challenge to all of *us,* too, not just to stand by and judge the morality of certain kinds of suicide, but to keep people from the kinds of losses that drive them to such desperation in the first place.

On the other hand, sometimes there are people whose pain is so intense and unavoidable that it seems hard to deny that death can be a considered and humane choice. Your heart goes out to them, and I for one know that in their situation I might well wish the same thing.

It's possible that many people on both sides would be willing to accept a policy that allowed assisted suicide under tightly controlled conditions. Several independent doctors would have to concur; waiting periods could be required; double and triple checks would be necessary to be sure patients were not just depressed; communities and governments would need to be sure that people in pain always have alternatives—but *then,* given all this, if people still resolutely seek to die, maybe it is time to respect their wishes. It may be possible, in short, to legalize assisted suicide in a limited way that both acknowledges the genuine dangers (fears of freelance "Doctor Deaths," like Kevorkian; dangers that it will become an "easy way out") while also recognizing that, sometimes at least, it can be a humane and proper choice.

You might be interested to know that just this kind of policy has been adopted in Oregon (and repeatedly reaffirmed by the voters), with results that, while still controversial, at least don't sound like an epidemic of suicides. About thirty people have secured permission for medically assisted death each year since the option became available.

"Owl versus Man"

Now consider the so-called "Owl versus Man" debate. Once again the first thing to say is that despite this polarized way of putting it, there are genuine values at stake on both sides.

The owls, on the one hand, are stand-ins for the values of the wild world, and specifically of the old-growth forests that are their only habitat. We respect their antiquity, their beauty, and indeed their sheer difference. We may even have the feeling that the possibility of our own lives being rich and rewarding is partly tied up with a richly varied natural world. On the other hand, we also care about preserving people's jobs and the communities that depend on the timber economy. We care about the quality of life that timber products make possible. Sometimes we do need wood!

To deny or shrug off either set of concerns in the name of the other does not contribute to a better understanding or to a just solution. Can we instead go ahead together?

We could try to compromise. Again, this is not irresponsible or morally weak, especially not if done well. Since so little old-growth forest is left, for example, the health of the timber industry hardly depends upon it. Maybe no more needs to be cut at all. Other places could be cut instead. In fact, both sides could sometimes "win" if land were *traded*—if more ecologically or aesthetically vital land were preserved by trading less vital land for it. Precisely this policy was adopted by the Clinton Interior Department and (although criticized by some on both sides) has managed to somewhat defuse the "timber wars" in recent years.

Once again, though, we should be able to do better still. There may be more integrative possibilities. If we could create jobs based on owl-watching tourism, for instance, as has been done very successfully with whales, then owl interests and human interests might *converge* rather than diverge.

Or again, we could seek to create a sustainable timber industry, using wood in a more intensive, craft-based way, rather than shipping massive amounts of raw wood abroad or pulping it for plywood, as the big timber corporations do at present. *That* kind of logging, unlike the present practice, would have a future: better for loggers *and* the forests.

Gun Control: A Dialogue

Thinking integratively takes some getting used to, and it's not always easy to stick to it, either, when you are dealing with people who picture moral debates only in polarized terms. Here's one example of how it might go in practice.

M: Are you for or against gun control?
P: Yes.

M: What do mean, "yes"? Yes or *no?* Which one? Whose side are you on?

P: I think that both sides are onto something. I favor some kinds of gun control, but I also think that gun control by itself partly misses the point.

M: In short, you don't really know what you think. Well, let me tell you . . .

P: I *do* know what I think. I think that both sides have some valid points. On the one hand, I think it's pretty clear that certain kinds of guns do much more harm than good: they make it too easy to kill, or are too prone to accidents. Nobody thinks young children should be dying in gun accidents. Banning or at least controlling certain kinds of guns would be a good start. . . .

M: So you're for gun control! But if you ban some kinds of weapons then sooner or later we're going to ban all of them! Just let me tell you . . .

P: I don't see why we can't stop wherever we choose. The law already says that you can't own an atomic bomb or a bazooka or a flame-thrower. We already have gun control! We already ban some weapons without banning all.

M: Well, anyway, guns don't kill people, people kill people.

P: That's just a slogan, not very clear either. But I agree that in a deeper way, guns are usually not the real problem. If that's what the slogan really means. Usually the real problem is people's willingness to use such violence against each other in the first place.

M: So you're against gun control! Your head's on straight after all.

P: I am *for* some effective strategies for reducing violence and accidental shootings. Sometimes that means gun control; but it also means trying to address the underlying causes of killing.

INTEGRATIVE STRATEGIES AT A GLANCE

- When truly opposite values conflict, we can at least *split the difference.*
- Different values may still be *compatible.* We can explore them with an eye to finding ways to satisfy both at the same time.
- Most disagreements are framed by deeper shared values. We can work from those shared values—from that *common ground*—toward jointly agreeable resolutions.

M: I'm having a hard time getting a handle on what you think. It seems like you want to satisfy everybody.

P: Oh, terrible! Can't both sides be onto something?

M: You can't satisfy everybody. Get serious!

P: I'll try again. You want the freedom to own hunting rifles and collector's items. I doubt that people are getting murdered by those kinds of guns, so I don't see why you can't keep them. But the pro-control side wants to ban the handguns that are used in most murders, and lead to the most accidents, and I don't see why we can't do that too. Meanwhile, neither you nor I wants to live in such a violent society, and I think if you really mean it about "people killing people," you'd be right there with me supporting the kinds of measures that might actually reduce violence. *You* get serious!

M: It's still wishy-washy. You need to take a stand.

P: I *am* taking a stand! I just don't think the only way to take a stand is to act like I have the whole truth to myself.

P and M obviously bring different assumptions about moral disagreements to this debate. P's attitude opens up the possibility of some genuine progress. Regions of disagreement will remain, of course—even fundamental disagreements. That's no reason not to try to do better everywhere else. There is plenty to do!

For Practice and Thinking ∿

Some Questions

Why do you think we polarize values? That is, why is it so tempting? Do you agree with the suggested explanations in this chapter? What else might be going on? What about *you*—how well can you resist the temptation? What are two or three practical ways in which you could help yourself and those around you to avoid polarizing values?

Practice

"Each side is right about *something*," I've insisted. Given our usual habits, it's a hard message to get. We're too used to debating polarized issues. Just the mere acknowledgment that the other side has some points needs a lot of practice.

So: identify your current position on some of the "hot-button" issues of the day. Now consider the opposite position—the other side or sides. Ask yourself *what the other side(s) is right about*—not wrong, but *right*. Where do you actually agree with them? What are their strongest and most important points?

It's tempting to answer by just summarizing what you think the other side thinks. That's helpful too, but the task here is to go farther. What do they think *that you think too?* What do you actually think they're right about? If you're in a group setting, a variation of this exercise is to make a list together of all of the relevant values that *both* (all) sides in some debate share, even if it seems at the beginning that none is shared at all. Usually you can come up with a very long list. That in itself should be surprising—and inspiring.

For a variation of this exercise, visit some parking lots and write down the bumper stickers on moral issues you see. Look for a wide range, including the ones that infuriate you. Now try to write alternative *integrative* bumper stickers. Is there a way to say something pithy that brings us together rather than divides us, that clarifies or connects rather than misrepresents and polarizes?

For example, you will discover a great deal of pro-choice and pro-life sloganizing. GOD HATES ABORTION, they say. ABORTION STOPS A BEATING HEART. On the other side, IF YOU'RE AGAINST ABORTION, DON'T HAVE ONE. So it was an inspiration one day to see EVERY CHILD A WANTED CHILD. Think of that: instead of trashing the other side for the evils of their ways, there is an appeal to the kind of value that unites us. It doesn't insist on one side over the other; it reminds us of what we should *all* aim for in the end. Every child a wanted child, which means: women have both the right and the responsibility to regulate pregnancy. Every child a wanted child, which means: when pregnancy occurs, we need to do everything we can to be sure the potential child *is* "wanted," that is, that the family can sustain the pregnancy and the child. The whole issue appears in a different light—and as a collective responsibility, an invitation to try to better the world.

Limits and Exceptions

Granting that there is something right about *most* sides of *most* debates, is this true of *all* sides in *all* debates? Is it always true that each side has a point?

I'm inclined to say yes, but then I've also been accused of being an overly generous person. What do *you* think?

Be careful not to say that there is nothing right about a certain moral position just because you disagree with its ultimate conclusion. Remember that people who draw different moral conclusions may still share many of the same moral values. They just balance them out differently. People who are pro-choice on abortion, for example, also value life—indeed probably value it very highly—but still believe that in at least some situations choice must take precedence. The value of life remains a shared value, and one good starting point for working together.

Generosity also suggests looking "underneath" a moral position, even one we find repugnant, to ask what genuine needs or concerns may be motivating it. For example, hatred against other, "outside" groups may arise out of a deep sense of exclusion and disempowerment. And this too, before it settles on some scapegoat, could be a perfectly valid feeling. Just repressing the advocates of such evils leaves the attraction of the evil itself untouched. Repression may even drive it deeper, making it more attractive. Even here, then—even when we can genuinely speak of right versus *wrong*—we need to try to listen, to try to figure out the other side rather than just condemning it outright, and to try to figure out how the people involved can be reached.

So again: can you think of any considered moral position that is just flat-out completely *wrong,* with nothing redeeming whatsoever to be said for it? Take some time and care with this question. It's not at all as easy as it might look, however you answer.

NOTES

The quote from John Dewey is from his essay "The Construction of Good," Chapter 10 of his book *The Quest for Certainty,* reprinted in James Gouinlock, *The Moral Writings of John Dewey* (Macmillan, 1976), Chapter 5, where the quotation can be found on p. 154. The general theme of integrating values is thoroughly Deweyan, as Gouinlock's collection makes clear. See also my book *Toward Better Problems* (Temple University Press, 1992), as well as *A 21st Century Ethical Toolbox,* Chapter 7.

Roger Fisher and William Ury's book *Getting to Yes* (Penguin, 1991) is essential practical reading on integrating values. Also useful is Tom Rusk, *The Power of Ethical Persuasion* (Penguin, 1993).

On compromise, a helpful philosophical treatment is Martin Benjamin's *Splitting the Difference* (University Press of Kansas, 1990). Benjamin systematically contests the various arguments that ethical philosophers have offered (or might offer—the arguments are seldom fully spelled out) against taking compromise seriously as a moral method. Given the plurality of values, Benjamin argues, what he calls "integrity-preserving compromise" is not only possible but sometimes even *required* in ethics.

Be careful not to reduce all integrative thinking to some form of compromise. Normally we can do much better than that. When compatible values are dovetailed, or when we work from common ground, we're not just "splitting the difference." Though the difference may remain, we may still be able to honor *all* of the values on both sides, to go much farther, as it were, than halfway. Compromise is nothing to be ashamed of, but it is still a kind of last resort. First there are more creative avenues to try.

Time's "Owl versus Man" cover appeared on 25 June 1990. For background on the integrative approach to "Owl versus Man" suggested in the text, see the accompanying article (which, interestingly, is not at all as polarized as the cover suggests) and John B. Judis, "Ancient Forests, Lost Jobs," *In These Times* 14:31 (Aug. 1-14, 1990). Environmental ethics is discussed in more detail in *Toolbox*, Chapter 21. A thorough study concluding that environmentalism and economic welfare are *not* at odds—that in fact they go together—is Stephen Meyer, *Environmentalism and Economic Prosperity* (MIT Project on Environmental Politics and Policy, 1992).

On the values involved with the assisted suicide debate, see Margaret Battin, Rosamond Rhodes, and Anita Silvers, *Physician-Assisted Suicide: Expanding the Debate* (Routledge, 1998). For a Catholic approach that highlights assisted suicide as a communal challenge, see Richard Gula, *Euthanasia: Moral and Pastoral Perspectives* (Paulist Press, 1994). For the application of Kant's ethical theory to the question of suicide, see his *Grounding for the Metaphysics of Morals,* James Ellington, trans: (Hackett, 1981), p. 36. Kant does not mean that we must live passively in the face of suffering— just that ending our lives to escape the suffering is not one of our moral options.

Secular ethical theories and traditional moral systems lie mostly outside the scope of this book. Certainly they have their uses as ways of articulating values; and they can make connections and open up vistas we otherwise would never reach. On the other hand, people sometimes appeal to theories to justify their favorite values and then try to rule the competing values out of court entirely. In this case, polarized values on the practical level are only restated, in a more formal, abstract, and thus more entrenched and resistant way, on the theoretical level. For a sobering discussion of this process at work in medical ethics, see Richard Zaner, *Ethics and the Clinical Encounter* (Prentice Hall, 1988), Chapter 1.

Chapters 5 and 6 of *Toolbox* discuss the role and possibilities of ethical theories in much more detail, though even there I can only scratch the surface. Some theories claim to assimilate all other values and moral principles under a single, all-inclusive criterion of value: these are usually the "utilitarian" theories that aim to maximize satisfaction or happiness as the ultimate good. Other theories claim priority for rights or duties, or perhaps the virtues. All of this is controversial, but it is safe to say that none of these theoretical claims has been firmly established. Ethical theories, though useful, still need to be approached with caution. Note that I am not at all arguing that theory itself must be rejected: the point is rather that it's wisest to let theories counterbalance and limit each other's claims. Multiplying perspectives on a single issue need not hinder problem-solving at all—quite the contrary, as this chapter has tried to argue.

5

THE ONGOING JOURNEY

Life tends to put new adventures and questions in our paths before we have even figured out the old ones. In ethics too: always there are new things to think about, new invitations to creativity and problem-solving together—the themes of this book so far.

My last theme is: make the most of it. Always seek to learn more, to see more deeply and clearly, to allow yourself and others to keep growing. Ethics cannot be a closed book or a finished product. The ethical life is an ongoing journey.

ETHICS AS A LEARNING EXPERIENCE

I ask my students what they've learned about ethical values in the last few years. A few say that little has changed. More say that not so much has changed yet, but they're looking forward to it. Most say that they *have* changed, ethically, often in ways they would never have predicted.

They travel, for fun maybe, but come back with whole new ideas about life. They learn about some new subject and have to change their ways. They have a friend or a family member who has an accident or a challenged child, and suddenly they have both more sympathy for others and more passion for the moment.

Even a few simple facts can change everything. Veal has a lovely taste, but when you learn what is done to veal calves, you may no longer wish to have any part of it. Farther down the same road you may realize that nearly all animals raised for meat are treated in similar ways—extreme confinement, frustration of natural instincts, and much worse too—and then meat itself becomes a moral question. No one really wants to think that something so widely enjoyed and widely available could also be a moral problem, but it may be so all the same. However we answer, it's a question we must deal with.

You learn not only new facts but also new habits. What if we really did start to approach ethical conflicts by asking what the "other side" is *right* about—what values we share? That would be a fairly dramatic kind of learning, don't you think?

Take up even the abortion issue, for instance, and instead of the all-too-familiar polarization of "pro-life" versus "pro-choice" we would look for common ground. Listen to the news or the usual debates, and you would think such a thing is not even possible, but there is already a national organization called "Search for Common Ground" sponsoring projects in which activists from *both* sides work *together* for common goals such as reducing the number of unwanted pregnancies in the first place.

The story of ethics itself is continuously unfolding. The idea of rights, for example, which most of us take for granted, is a piece of ethical theory that was literally revolutionary in the eighteenth century. On July 4th we shoot off fireworks and celebrate the Declaration of Independence as if it were the most natural and obvious thing. But it was a radical document in its time—after all, it started a *revolution*—and even now we struggle to realize the full promise of "all [people] are created equal."

Meantime we are also beginning to see Declarations of *Inter*dependence: the insistence that we humans are deeply dependent on the rest of the biosphere for our health, wealth, and very survival—and that it would therefore be a good idea to treat nature with more respect. Even something as simple as recycling, for example, did not cross people's minds for generations, but it will surely be part of any sustainable earth ethic in the future.

More of the same is surely coming down the road. More revolutionary issues will come up, such as an entire range of thorny and unprecedented questions about cloning and genetic engineering. Old issues will come up in new forms, such as questions about privacy rights in an age preoccupied with security. In personal and professional life, "just getting by" by current standards is soon likely to be nowhere near enough. Ethical norms for managers and CEOs are changing so fast that some of yesterday's accepted behavior is already becoming grounds for dismissal. Stop learning, and the world will pass you by.

LOOKING FARTHER

Really, though, we are challenged to do more than simply keep up. Understand ethics as an ongoing journey, and it also becomes part of our challenge to think *ahead* of the curve— not merely to follow along but to think carefully about the ways we should go.

Learning More

Even a few simple facts, I said, can change everything. It follows that part of our responsibility is to *seek out* the facts—

honestly and persistently. We need to do more than simply assert what we think is "obvious," or seek out a few facts that seem to support what we already think. The real challenge is to find out more, to understand better, even if what we think may have to change as a result.

Is global warming actually happening—what does the best science say? Do children raised by gay couples grow up sexually confused (any more than the average adolescent)? Is "restorative justice"—reconciliation rather than retribution—possible? How much do animals suffer in laboratories and slaughterhouses? Who actually is on welfare? Do homeless people tend to be drug addicts (or is it that drug addicts tend to be homeless)?

All of these questions are primarily factual. That is, actual evidence is available, though it can be complex and uncertain at times. Many of these questions have been the subjects of thorough study. You can find some answers—but it does take looking.

Keep your eyes open, too. Remember that, in ethics in particular, strong opinions may color the facts. Certainly they color *presentations* of the facts. So use a variety of sources, use sources that are as reliable as you can find, carefully check the citations for any factual claims that are central to your argument or seem debatable, and watch the reasoning, especially if the argument makes statistical claims or claims about causes. The notes to this chapter suggest a few helpful argument guides.

Check out even those claims you think are obvious. If they're central to serious moral disagreements, then they're pretty likely *not* obvious to others. In any case, you need some evidence. Are corporations solely driven by the bottom line? Does the death penalty deter would-be murderers? Does gun control? What would happen if marijuana were legalized? Opinion is not enough!

Broadening Experience

Just as important as seeking the facts is broadening our *experience*, especially of others we know only indirectly and through the screen of our own reactions: people who disagree with us, people who are different, people who make us uncomfortable. When we fly by stereotype and prejudice, the result is that we miss the depth of things. We can do better.

Seek out experiences that will ground you in the real worlds of others. Don't presume to judge lesbians or career soldiers or "today's youth" or anyone else (foreigners, cops, teenagers, corporate managers, poor people, rich people, the depressed, activists of all stripes . . .) until you actually know a few. Or more than a few.

Remind yourself that you do not know everything there is to know about a person just on the basis of his or her appearance or a few labels. I have learned more from my mentally retarded brother than from many of my teachers. But to most people he is just "retarded." They can't see past the labels. Likewise, no one is just a "liberal" or a lawyer or a fundamentalist—any more than *you* could be reduced to such a label. Be prepared to look farther. And be prepared for surprises.

My ethics classes help staff a shelter for homeless people near our college. We go into the shelter with anxieties, self-conscious, carrying the culture's baggage of images and media stereotypes. We come out seeing something different. One student wrote after her first visit:

> All of my insecurities were running through my head as I approached the door and had to be let in by one of the guests. Some people were gathered by the TV and it's funny to me now, but the first thing I thought was "Hey, I watch that show too!" It's embarrassing to look back now at how nervous I was

because then it hit me that homeless people are just the same as me. . . . Right away I was so glad I had come.

Other students meet people who remind them of their grand-mothers or friends—and themselves. They learn that most of the residents (this shelter calls them "guests") work, and that many have two or even three jobs—but are still stuck in the shelter. Some students are brought up short when they assume that a well-dressed person in the shelter must be another volunteer—only to find that he or she is a guest. "At that moment," says one, "I realized that I too could be here. . . . "

While you're at it, be careful not to sell *yourself* short, either. We get used to a way of living—maybe it's the only way we've known—and then it is hard to imagine ourselves living any other way. For most of my life I could not imagine being a parent, but now parenting has become a joy and a constant stimulation, and I cannot imagine *not* being a parent. And I doubt I'm done learning in this way. Could I even become a pilgrim in later life, in the Jain way, leaving my present life behind? And what about you? Could you live just as well, or better, on a much tinier income? Or: what if everything you did was environmentally sustainable? How do you really know until you've ventured, at least in some small way, to try?

Opening Possibilities

Seeking facts, broadening experience . . . but there is also another way in which we must "look farther." It requires a commitment to *opening possibilities* as well.

Sometimes the challenge is to find room in some problem that until now has seemed totally stuck. Reframing "the" drug problem, for example, to ask how we might make life so exciting that escape through drugs is less tempting in the first place. Remaking certain kinds of "litter" as food, maybe, so that people could just finish off the bottles and wrappers after eating the contents, like taco shells and ice cream cones—no more litter problem! "Out of the box" solutions like these don't present themselves within the problem itself. Creative thinking must, well, create them. It's a step beyond just seeking the facts: we must be willing to think in a more active and indeed visionary way too.

We are also invited to think in a more visionary way about each *other*. Again it may require going beyond "the facts" of the moment—but now in a rather different way. This is because moral devaluation can have a self-confirming character.

When someone treats me dismissively or mistrustfully, my behavior changes too. I become mistrustful myself, or angry and impatient—very likely confirming just the view of me that led to my being dismissed or mistrusted in the first place. A certain circle closes. I'm locked in. Approaching in the opposite way, though, I might well have been a very different person.

Whole lives can be "locked in" like this. Children who are considered stupid from the start, for example, naturally come to see themselves the same way. And for both this reason and the lack of serious social investment in their educations, they may well *become* less intelligent. To those who didn't see (or refuse to recognize) the denial, they will simply seem stupid by nature—and therefore it's lucky we didn't waste schooling on them, isn't it?

It can be hard to keep the real causes straight when the actual children with all their deficiencies are here before our eyes. That's where the vision comes in: it's a step beyond just seeking the facts, again, because we are required to think critically about how "the facts" *came about*—and to make changes as needed. For here too a different approach might produce a different response. Teachers who actually believe in their students' possibilities can awaken something that no one else—not even the students themselves—had seen before. The point is that the teachers have to take the first step. They have to offer trust and an invitation up front. And what if society did so too?

So reach out to others. Say hello to people on the street, and see what kind of goodwill comes back to you. Offer a troubled child or a troubled friend some love or trust, rather than just moralizing in the hopes that maybe someday he or she will deserve it. Try treating others—all others, even and especially those you have come to fear or despise or dismiss— as actual human beings. See what kinds of responses come back *then*.

THE EXPANDING CIRCLE

Ethics is changing in part because the circle of our ethical concern continues to grow. While some of us still struggle with the idea that ethics applies equally to *everyone*—rich and poor, young and old, fellow citizen and foreigner—others are beginning to look beyond the borders of the human species itself. Here is one of those places where ethics is both especially challenging and especially intriguing.

Other Animals

We are used to thinking of other animals as lesser creatures, indeed hardly as creatures at all—more like mere resources to serve our needs. Commercially raised chickens spend the whole of their short lives in cages too small to even allow them to turn around. Veal calves are deprived of nutrients, exercise, even light. Large numbers of dogs, chimps, cats, rabbits, and many other animals are used each year to test new drugs and chemicals.

Yet we are also beginning to have questions. Confronted with what actually happens in "factory farms," we are at least uneasy, maybe outraged. We may begin to recognize a certain "lock-in" here too. Animals who are treated like living egg or milk machines, or living pieces of meat, genuinely *become* unsociable, incapable, and pitiful—not to mention dangerous to themselves and others. People who know such animals are often genuinely puzzled that anyone would have any ethical issues with how they are treated—the animals seem so pitiful. But the very fact that the animals are reduced to such a state is itself an issue. They are *made* pitiful. We only barely glimpse their other possibilities.

People are changing, too. Vegetarianism is on the rise, most restaurants now serve nonmeat dishes, and even people who continue to eat meat are beginning to feel obliged to make excuses for it, which is at least a sign that they feel some unease. Others are seeking to honor and recover human companionship with a wide variety of other species. Still others are creating new forms of human-animal relation: musicians, for example, who jam with orcas. At the very least, we're no longer willing simply to dismiss other animals. We're beginning to *notice*.

Animals can't think, some people say. They don't feel pain, and on and on. But we are learning—or remembering—another and truer story. In her essay "Am I Blue?" Alice Walker writes of a horse who came to live in a field near her home. The horse—Blue—visits her apple tree, and she starts paying attention. The first thing she sees is that

> Blue was lonely. Blue was horribly lonely and bored. . . . Five acres to tramp by yourself, endlessly, even in the most beauti-

ful of meadows . . . cannot provide many interesting events, and once rainy season turned to dry that was about it. . . . I had forgotten that human animals and nonhuman animals can communicate quite well; if we are brought up around animals as children we take this for granted. It is in [animals'] nature to express themselves. What else are they going to express? And, generally speaking, they are ignored.

Now Walker starts making connections. She begins to muse on the parallels to the treatment of black slaves, Indians, and sometimes the young: ignored too. The very possibility that they might have something of their own to communicate is often denied. Too often we see only our own reflections in those we subordinate and oppress.

Walker travels for a time. When she returns, Blue has a companion. "There was a new look in his eyes. A look of independence, of self-possession, of inalienable *horseness.*" There are weeks of a deep and mutual feeling of justice and peace. But eventually Blue's companion becomes pregnant: it turns out that she was "put with him" (a phrase also used for slaves) for that purpose. Then she is taken away.

Blue was like a crazed person. Blue *was*, to me, a crazed person. He galloped furiously . . . around and around his five acres. He whinnied until he couldn't. He tore the ground with his hooves. . . . He looked always and always toward the road down which his partner had gone. And then, occasionally . . . , he looked at me. It was a look so piercing, so full of grief, a look so *human*, that I almost laughed (I felt too sad to cry) to think there are people who do not know animals suffer.

But they do. Again Walker is led to think about the suffering all around us and about how too often we evade or deny that communication. The conclusion then is quick and stunning:

As we talked of freedom and justice one day for all, we sat down to steaks. I am eating misery, I thought, as I took the first bite. And spit it out.

Having come to see her own actions in a different light, the result was that at that moment Walker stopped eating meat.

It's important to add that you or I might have responded differently. After all, there's no direct connection between how Blue was treated and the production of steaks. But Walker's essay follows a much bigger track. By compelling us to see Blue as a real, feeling being, she raises the question of animals in *general* in an unforgettable way. It is now, unavoidably, one of the ethical questions of the times.

A New Earth Ethic

Ethics is also trying to respond to environmental crisis. We know that we need to cut back on pollution, reduce waste, save endangered species. We need to keep air and water clean so we can breathe and drink in good health. Save the rainforests—maybe we will find the cure for cancer there.

Less familiar values are also often at stake with the environment. Justice often requires environmental respect, for example. Much environmental damage is also damage to other human communities. Rainforest destruction displaces whole forest communities. Whole cultures are being driven into extinction. Strip-mining, drift-netting, toxic-waste dumping—all of these immediately and profoundly affect *us* too.

So environmental ethics may well call for radical changes. We may need to cut way back on ozone-depleters and automobiles and so many kinds of waste we now just take for granted. If it's really true in nature that "what goes around comes around," then we need to be a lot more careful about what "goes around"!

There's more, though. Ethics itself may also be changing in the process. In part, of course, taking care of nature is a way of taking care of ourselves. Here the appeal is to *human* values: health, justice, and so on. But could it be that there are also other reasons to care about nature? Mightn't we be beginning to recognize that nature also has some claim in its own right—that the ethical world, like the actual living world, is *bigger than we are?*

Some people have begun to say that endangered species have a right to exist just for themselves. Not just for us. Spotted owls, blue whales, even certain endangered bats and tiny, out-of-the-way fish—these are co-travelers with us through the eons. In religious terms, they are just as much a part of Creation as we are. It is wrong to drive them off the earth just for some small convenience to ourselves, or perhaps solely out of thoughtlessness. They have as much right to be here as we do. So may wild rivers and forests and mountains—they have a right to remain in their natural states.

So new visions are emerging, and with them the possibilities of whole new ethics. We are beginning to recognize the enormous creativity, complexity, and depth of the rest of the world: the nonhuman, the other-than-human, the more-than-human. The grandeur and magic of nature, the silence-that-is-not-stillness of the wild, the glittering stars, birds everywhere, the very continents gliding about on oceans of molten rock, and on and on. Part of the ethical lesson may be that other values call to us besides purely human values—and that it is time (*past* time) to answer the call. And so the circle keeps expanding.

Again, then: ethics is an ongoing journey, both in our own lives and in our larger communities and society. In fact, this is part of what makes it so difficult—and so exciting. Stay with it. And keep both an open heart and an open mind.

FOR PRACTICE AND THINKING ~

Inspirations

Look for biographies or autobiographies of people you admire ethically. Pay attention to the ways in which they learned and changed. How did they become the people they are? What made moral learning and change possible for them?

Interview some people you know or could contact, asking the same questions. What have been major ethical changes in their lives? Why did those changes happen? Were they hard? Why? How do these people feel about the changes now that they look back at them from some distance? What advice do they have for younger people—you, for example—looking ahead to such changes in their own lives?

Looking Ahead

How do you think ethics will look in, say, a hundred years? For example, what do you think ethics will be saying about animals in a hundred years? About the natural world? And what will be the farther frontiers of ethics if these areas become more familiar? Outer space? Bioengineering?

Take the question of environmental ethics. I have suggested, in effect, that environmental ethics is in a very early stage of development. We might hope that in a hundred years we'll be a little farther along—and again, not just in the sense that people will be more aware of and committed to environmental responsibility, but that ethics itself will respond directly to the call of nature, not just indirectly through various human-oriented values. But what will an ethics of this sort look like? How will it describe the new, beyond-the-human values?

Correspondingly, what values do you think will *not* change? (And why not?)

Make Some Changes Yourself

Service is an unparalleled form of ethical learning—not to mention a prime way of putting ethics into action. Find a way to help that is genuinely face-to-face. Volunteer at a local homeless shelter or soup kitchen or struggling elementary school. Work with the physically or mentally challenged. Teach a class at a community center or a nursing home. Help build a house with Habitat for Humanity. Push your envelope.

The mechanics are usually easy. Making the arrangements takes only a phone call. Most homeless shelters, for instance, are desperate for volunteer help and have staff coordinators to arrange volunteers' dates and times. When floods or storms strike, many cities or counties set up volunteer hotlines to match willing volunteers with people in need of help. Community newspapers often run appeals for help. School offices schedule community volunteers and tutors. Most colleges have offices that match community organizations' needs and student volunteers. Find yours and use it.

There are other ethical experiments you might try. Try a retreat in total silence. Check out a vegetarian group on campus or in your area. Seek out a few improbable friendships—who knows what might come of them? Pay attention to some of your habits, and try some changes. For example, spend a day (or a week) responding only positively to people, no matter how they approach you. Do your interactions change as a result?

NOTES

Once again, check out my *21st Century Ethical Toolbox* for more on all of these themes. See Chapter 1 on ethics as a learning experience; Chapter 3 on paying attention to values; Chapter 15 on service; and Chapters 20–21 on "the expanding circle." Chapters 8–10 delve into critical thinking in ethics.

There is a wide variety of available textbooks in critical thinking. A new one I especially like is Lewis Vaughn's *The Power of Critical Thinking* (Oxford, 2005). For starters in this area, there is also my own little guide, *A Rulebook for Arguments* (Hackett Publishing Company, 2001).

You can find Search for Common Ground on the web at <www.searchforcommonground.org>. For more on an integrative approach to the abortion issue, see *Toolbox* Chapter 17 and the reading from Roger Rosenblatt in Chapter 7.

The image of an expanding ethical circle was introduced by Peter Singer in a book by the same title: *The Expanding Circle* (Farrar, Straus, and Giroux, 1981). Singer's *Animal Liberation* (revised edition, Ecco, 2001), along with Tom Regan's *The Case for Animal Rights* (University of California Press, 1983) and Mary Midgley's *Animals and Why They Matter* (University of Georgia Press, 1983) are classic philosophical defenses of the ethical status of other animals. Alice Walker's "Am I Blue?" is cited from her collection *Living by the Word* (Harcourt Brace Jovanovich, 1988).

On the extension of ethics to the whole of the ecosphere, the classic source is Aldo Leopold, *Sand County Almanac* (Oxford University Press, 1949). The opening of the last essay in that book, "The Land Ethic," also calls upon the image of an expanding circle. For a next step, try my *An Invitation to Environmental Philosophy* (Oxford University Press, 1999), and be sure to consult the extensive bibliography at the end.

APPENDIX

Writing an Ethics Paper

This book presents ethics primarily as a mode of action, and accordingly we have been concerned with practical skills. In school, though, ethics is usually taught as a subject matter, and one of the primary skills called into play is *writing*. This Appendix therefore offers some guidelines for writing an ethics paper.

FOUR KINDS OF WRITING IN ETHICS

A variety of kinds of writing can be appropriate in ethics. Each has a different and somewhat distinctive goal; each therefore calls for a rather different kind of project.

1. Exploring an Issue

It may be that some moral value or some moral issue intrigues you, and you want to know more about it. Maybe you want to understand how people can come to take animals so seriously, like Alice Walker, that they stop eating them. Or maybe you want to know what a certain moral debate—genetic engineering? affirmative action?—is all about. Just to understand these things is enough—and, often, *hard* enough—all by itself.

Remember that not all moral exploration needs to be an *argument*. Walker, for instance, is not outlining her reasoning or considering counterarguments or doing all of the other things she'd need to do to nail down a "position." She's just telling her *story*—letting us in on the ways in which her heart and her thoughts moved. You may wish to tell your own story, or explore someone else's, in the same way.

Even when you are exploring a moral debate, you are not obliged to join it. You can survey the different positions, trying to understand them all, without taking one. Of course, joining a debate is one way to explore it, but it is certainly not the only way. You may also choose a more open-ended kind of exploration in which you (and, maybe, your classmates) look into all of the relevant values, factual arguments, and options without feeling personally committed to one view or the other. Explore first, commit later—if you have to commit at all.

2. Getting Unstuck

Another possible goal is to get yourself or a group or a community past some of the sticking points in a debate as it stands. Here you want to draw specifically on your creative skills.

Take on a real issue, an issue where you can make an actual contribution. Consider live controversies in your school community or hometown. Watch for public comment meetings on local, state, or national policy matters. Go to the meetings or visit the websites. Look at the editorials and letters to the editor in local and state newspapers. Ask: What kinds of contributions would actually help? Where is the debate stuck at present?

In particular, we are often stuck over options. We think we don't have many. As Chapter 3 points out, we tend to speak of moral "dilemmas," as if we expect moral problems to always take the shape of two opposed and fairly unsatisfactory options. Gun control, abortion, capital punishment—on issues such as these a few polarized options dominate our thinking. More specific controversies are often similar.

You have the tools now to get debates like these *un*stuck. You can multiply options and reframe problems. You can also look to the contending values with an eye toward finding common ground or compatible values or at least acceptable compromises. You can pay careful attention to *all* the values at stake and help both sides acknowledge values that, in the midst of a polarized debate, they may have trouble even hearing.

Notice that in this case you are not arguing for or against a position, either. You elect to serve instead as a creative facilitator, trying to take account of all of the contending arguments and positions. This is a worthy role too. It is rarely enough done well, or done at all, that it can be a first-rate contribution—sometimes the most vital contribution of all.

3. Making a Case

Then again, you may *want* (or be required) to take one side in a moral debate and defend it. Maybe you will be taking part in a public debate on some moral topic and will be assigned or will choose one "side" to defend. Or perhaps you will be assigned an ethics paper to write in an argumentative style.

Here you want to advance the kinds of values and factual arguments that will persuade others to join your cause. You want to give those values an eloquent voice; to trace a compelling and natural path from those values to the course of action you are defending; and to show that the concerns others have raised about it (that is, objections to your case) are not the serious drawbacks the objectors claim they are. Even so, of course, you don't want to overlook good points on the other side(s) or "win" by playing on others' emotions or misrepresenting the known facts. Public argument—making a case—is not a game for its own sake. It's still in service of finding the best way, together. Tracing a path from compelling values back to practical action can do just that.

Making a case is probably the most common writing assignment in ethics, so I will say more about it in a separate section.

4. Deciding for Yourself

Some moral problems confront us with a personal urgency. A nurse may believe that she owes all of her patients the same high level of care. On the other hand, she may also fear for herself when regularly in contact with patients who have very dangerous diseases. So sometimes she is tempted to withhold the touch, to keep her distance, yet that may feel as wrong as rushing headlong into the risk. How should she decide?

Or again: Do you work honestly when others around you are getting ahead by cutting corners? Blow the whistle on others who are cutting corners? Use drugs? Support the latest war?

A paper may aim to answer this sort of question. Here your goal is not just to explore the issue, and it is not to make a constructive contribution to a larger debate (though that may also happen). You are not making a case, either, in the sense that you are not talking about policies or general positions. The aim is to decide a question for yourself: to take a stand, to settle the question, for now at least, for *you*. You must decide what you yourself, at least, should do.

You still need to start with some exploration, though. Don't prejudge the issue—the point is not to rationalize a decision you've already made. Look carefully at the values involved on all sides. As Chapter 5 urges, try to learn more, broaden your experience, take seriously possibilities that may at first be closed off. Ask around: get other people's advice. People you know have probably been in very similar circumstances. What did they choose? How did it work out? Are there other people whose advice has always been helpful: minister or rabbi, parent, friend?

See if you can find unexpected or imaginative ways around or through the problem. Look for creative middle ground between the contending values. Our nurse, for example, might try to get very specific about the *real* dangers (often much less or more specific than our vague and broad fears tell us) and seek to find a sensitive and respectful way to deal with those few patients who actually might pose a threat.

MAKING A CASE

In making a case, you are not being asked simply to provide an elaborate rationalization for your preexisting opinion. You are being asked to *think*—and to help your reader think with you.

Be Specific

Begin by being as clear as you can about what exactly the question is. Get specific. Maybe you really do want to argue about "poverty" generally, in its many dimensions. On the other hand, maybe what you really want to consider is whether or not there should be a certain kind of governmental welfare program. That is quite different!

Carefully lay out what your case is actually for. Be specific and don't overstate. It is not enough to answer "abortion," say, or "sexual freedom." If you wish to defend abortion, what you probably wish to defend is keeping abortion legal under certain circumstances. Specify the circumstances. Will there still be limits, for example? What limits? Why? If you are opposed to abortion, also say what you're *for*. A little precision at this point makes things a lot simpler later on.

Name the Key Values

Make your key values explicit. What are the most fundamental reasons supporting your position? If a specific proposal is involved, what is the basic need it meets or value it promotes? Be explicit about the underlying moral values. Your other readings in ethics should help you here: they will lay out a language, and perhaps also some theories or systems of ethics, to help define general values and ethical principles.

Be aware that just naming the moral values you are calling upon can be a powerful move. Too often we feel embarrassed to publicly declare ourselves for certain values, and so we leave them unspoken and "stick to the facts." This may be reasonable enough when the implicit values favor your side, though even then it is better to be explicit. Often, though, the implicit values in public debates are only the most basic and self-serving—while the values that need to be spoken for are sometimes more subtle and easily overlooked. In that case, you have to be explicit. Other things matter too: it's up to you to point them out.

Be careful not to ignore or dismiss the other side. Figure out *why* other people disagree—when they do. Showing that you understand and can even appreciate their position helps to establish your own credibility too. If you yourself haven't considered the matter carefully enough to have explored the other positions, why should the rest of us take your arguments seriously?

Maybe the "other side" has different values. In that case it is respectful at least to acknowledge them. Remember that you can still seek common ground and ways in which even sharply different values can be compatible. Other times, you may actually *share* basic values, but disagree about the facts. In that case it is especially powerful to start on the values side: you make it clear that the disagreement is not actually a moral disagreement at all. Disagreements over whether, say, how well a policy will work are quite different, and often much more approachable, than disagreements over whether it serves the right values.

Unfold the Argument

Now lay out and defend the key factual claims your case needs to succeed. Cite the strongest sources you can; spell out your key inferences and your basis for them clearly; clarify and define any problematic terms. Make it clear too that you have thought carefully about other options. A good case must show that its position or proposal is the *best response* to the problem or need that motivates your case.

Suppose you want to defend the death penalty. Maybe you want to claim that it has a deterrence effect. This may seem "obvious," but a little research will show you that the data are actually unclear on this point. States with the death penalty often have higher murder rates than states that don't, which is the opposite of what the "obvious" theory predicts, though you might also wonder whether those states would have had still higher murder rates without the death penalty. At the very least, you need to do some serious work to find useful data—and put your conclusions very carefully.

There's also more to show. No doubt the death penalty is a better deterrent than doing nothing at all. But the question is whether it deters murders *better than alternative punishments*—for example, whether it deters murders better than, say, an automatic life sentence without parole. An alternative case could even go farther and propose required community service as a form of restitution, which might be just as effective a deterrent while also drawing better on some additional values, like respect for life (the state wouldn't be in the business of killing people; and restitution would allow even murderers a chance to redeem themselves). Is the death penalty better than *that*? Maybe, but it takes some showing.

Be sure you are judging like cases alike. The stronger and clearer your position, the more directly it will invite comparison to other situations where your arguments might also apply. If you oppose the death penalty, why not abortion? If you're "pro-life" on abortion, are you also "pro-life" on issues of militarism, welfare, environment? There are no automatic and simple answers to these kinds of challenges, but, logically, they need to be considered.

Finally, you need to directly acknowledge and respond to the most important *objections* to your position or proposal. Any case worth making has a downside too. After all, in making a case you join an ongoing debate, and there are other sides too: again, other moral values of concern, other beliefs about the facts, and so on. No complete case can ignore such difficulties or simply dismiss the sorts of reasons that people might object to its proposal or favor some other position. So:

where do the problems lie? What will the chief objections be? Outline them and respond. Check out and back up the chief factual claims if necessary. Again analyze sources and inferences. Maybe you even have to change your own position! Acknowledge conflicts of values that the proposal may create. Can you use integrative strategies or more creative thinking to address some of these new problems?

TWO QUICK EXAMPLES

Whatever kind of paper you write, you want to make your paper itself *ethical*—not just a paper *about* ethics. Avoid polarizing values and dismissing positions or values other than yours. Convey an open mind through your willingness to reframe problems and seek common ground. Seek to contribute and not just to judge.

Two very short sample essays may help clarify the possibilities. Here is one on the subject of ethics and the elderly.

Let's Spend Medical Dollars More Wisely

I have heard that half of all the Medicare money spent in America goes to provide medical care for people in the very last stages of life, in the last two months of life. This is not a wise pattern, and it needs to change.

This spending does not occur in a vacuum. Money spent for end-state medical care could also be spent in other ways. Many other people have medical needs that are not being met: for instance, people who could get a heart transplant or bypass surgery, and live long and productive lives. The tough fact is that we do die eventually and trying to fight it off for the last few months just is not worth it to society.

Maybe a three-year-old child needs a kidney transplant to live. But there is no kidney available because the last one just went to a ninety-year-old patient who is barely able to get around on her own and is already senile. The ninety-year-old may have Medicare to pay for the surgery, or may have good medical insurance. The three-year-old's family may not have the money to pay for medical care, and the organ may not be available anyway. This is not right. We have to recognize that some lives are more valuable than others. When you've lived a long and full life, then it's just time to go.

People do die eventually. We need to get used to that fact and stop acting like we can put it off forever. My uncle died on a respirator after his cancers made him unable to talk or do anything, even stay awake. Still, he wanted everything possible to be done. Meanwhile, who knows what other person could have benefitted from all that medical attention?

Caps or ceilings could be put on how much surgery and other medical care is done for the really old, per year or per hospital or something. That would be a start. But still, they would have to recognize that there are other people with needs too, and we just have to make the hard choice to put our money where it will do the most good. We can't all live forever!

This essay has some strengths. It's direct—no beating around the bush. The writing is clear and punchy. It's concrete: it gives examples, and the examples are on the point.

But—a very big "but"—you can do better than this. In general, this is a high-opinion, low-support piece of writing on an issue that invites much more careful consideration. It's also rather dismissively written on an issue that calls for much more care.

From the very first line this essay is careless about the facts. Just because the writer has *heard* that half of all the Medicare money spent in America goes to provide medical care for people in the very last stages of life, is that claim therefore true? That claim is key to the essay and needs to be investigated, with a more exact number cited—and referenced. Likewise, how common really is it for younger people in need to be bumped by very old people with better resources? The essay implies that it is common, but the examples are just hypothetical. The writer does not seem to have gone to the trouble of actually checking it out. Not enough!

Moreover, the essay tends to repeat itself—even in its very short length—rather than *developing* its argument. The middle three paragraphs all make the same point in almost the same way. But there's much more to be worked out. "Putting our money where it does the most good," what's "worth it to society"—fair enough, but how are "good" and "worth" to be assessed here? Is "good" to be measured solely by longevity, for instance? Maybe, but it needs some argument. Aren't any other values in play? What about honoring elders?

Put another way, a paper in *ethics* must at some point turn the spotlight directly onto basic values and give them some attention in their own right. This paper walks up to that point—several times—but doesn't take the crucial step.

Finally, the tone is dismissive. "It's just time to go" isn't exactly a considerate piece of advice. And the essay overstates. Do we really act as though "we can put [death] off forever"? Phrases like these make the paper feel like a brush-off by someone who has not seriously or sympathetically engaged the question and does not feel at stake with it, either. It has a good point—patterns of end-state care *are* troubling, and perhaps we *do* need to redirect some of this care toward people whom it would benefit longer—but we need to explore these questions in a more constructive spirit. You can do better!

Here is a second sample essay on a related theme.

Ethics and Aging: What Can We Do?

Writing about older people is hard for people my age. We're young—so not only it is hard to imagine how life will feel at the other end, we also do not really want to. For one thing, they remind us of death, which we'd rather not think about. . . .

Different and even conflicting values are involved. The whole society sees the old as a little bit funny (not anything like ourselves, of course!): slow, opinionated, not so good at anything newfangled, stuck in the old ways—we all know the stereotypes. We want to be free of them. On the other hand, the old are our parents and grandparents, our teachers and their teachers. We respect them because they are the ones who gave us life and everything else that we have. All traditional cultures honor and revere the old, and for good reason.

As for us, though some part of us certainly shares the traditional reverence, in practice we tend to push the old to the edges of the action. Families live at too great distances and have their own over-full lives: so the older parent, perhaps having lost a spouse, ends up in a nursing home or trying to keep things together on their own.

I believe that ethics asks more of us than this. No one should end their life abandoned and alone, left to the care of strangers and professionals and possibly abuse too. These are real people, just like us—and we will be them, someday—and they have done their part. Yes, the younger generations need their chance and their freedom too, but we ought to ask how we can meet our needs without short-changing the needs of others.

We should explore some creative options. For example, part of the problem of abandonment, the loneliness of the old, is that old people's homes are cut off from the rest of their communities. There is no need for this! Old people's homes could be at the center of community life: the old are the ones who have time to spend with the young ones, for one thing. They can start the seedlings for gardens, they could staff the library and the historical museums, they can teach what they know. Rather than pushing them aside, society needs to brainstorm how the old can remain a vital part of life.

Even really old people can be enormously productive and active. One of my best dance teachers is in her 80s and more limber than most of the class. The architect Frank Lloyd Wright designed some of his best buildings in his 90s. Often it's when people lose their community, their friends, contact, and stimulation that they grow stale and stuffy. Sure, brains age too, but a lot of senility may really be a social problem. If they can stay more active, they will also stay more alert and involved. And there we can surely help!

This is a much better essay for its length. It clearly surveys the whole problem: from why we can be inattentive or closed-minded on this subject, through some of the variety of values involved, to some unexpected options. About each aspect it carries us a little farther beyond where the debate is carried on at present. The first essay was very short but at the same time very repetitive. This one is slightly longer, but not repetitive at all. Every paragraph takes a new step.

At the same time, this second essay's conclusions are not necessarily incompatible with the harder-nosed recommendations of the first. Maybe we do have to rein in medical spending at the very end of life. But that is not the essential question for the second paper. The second essay looks at a bigger picture: the *quality of life* of older people, rather than just end-state medical care. It is more concerned with the availability of human community to older people than with the availability of organs for transplant.

Notice even the contrast of titles. The title of the first essay suggests a judgment or a management decision—appropriate sometimes, but not the whole story. The title of the second asks us to engage *ourselves*. Go back and look at the last lines of each essay, too. The first essay ends by closing a door; the second ends by opening one. Let your writing open doors as well!

RESOURCES

For a range of models of good writing in ethics, check out teaching anthologies such as Lawrence Hinman's *Contemporary Moral Issues: Diversity and Consensus* (Prentice Hall, 2005) and Christina Hoff Sommers and Fred Sommers, *Vice and Virtue in Everyday Life* (Wadsworth Publishing, 2003). You can also find a range of examples among the readings in my book *A 21st Century Ethical Toolbox* (Oxford, 2001). Chapter 1 includes an interview by Studs Terkel with a former leader of the Ku Klux Klan who becomes an antiracist and labor organizer. Chapter 3 offers Edward Abbey's paean to "The Great American Desert." There is Roger Rosenblatt's attempt to mediate the abortion debate in Chapter 7, Colin McGinn's wild analogies concerning the treatment of other species in Chapter 10, an essay on trying to be a feminist man by Jason Schultz in Chapter 16, one on ending an afflicted pregnancy by Rayna Rapp in Chapter 17, and others too.

Chapter 13 of *Toolbox* offers more detailed advice about setting goals for different kinds of writing in ethics. General writing guides may also be helpful. Read enough of Natalie Goldberg's *Writing Down the Bones* (Shambhala, 1986), for instance, to get some inspiration and some good advice.

On persuasively entering the realm of public argument, see Annette Rottenberg, *Elements of Argument: A Text and Reader* (Bedford Press/St. Martin's, 2002), and Timothy Crusius and Carolyn Channell, *The Aims of Argument: A Rhetoric and Reader* (Mayfield, 2003). A useful and inspiring book on our potential contributions as citizens is Frances Moore Lappe and Paul Martin Dubois, *The Quickening of America: Rebuilding Our Nation, Remaking Our Lives* (Jossey-Bass, 1994).